Meeting Customer Needs

Ian Smith

Published in association with the Institute of Management

the Institute of Management
FOUNDATION

BUTTERWORTH
HEINEMANN

Butterworth-Heinemann Ltd
Linacre House, Jordan Hill, Oxford OX2 8DP

 A member of the Reed Elsevier group

OXFORD LONDON BOSTON
MUNICH NEW DELHI SINGAPORE SYDNEY
TOKYO TORONTO WELLINGTON

First published 1994

British Library Cataloguing in Publication Data
Smith, Ian
  Meeting Customer Needs. – (Institute of
  Management Foundation Series)
  I. Title II. Series
  658.8
ISBN 0 7506 0668 1

Composition by Genesis Typesetting, Laser Quay, Rochester, Kent
Printed and bound in Great Britain by Clays Ltd, St Ives plc

Meeting Customer Needs

Contents

Series adviser's preface

This book is one of a series designed for people wanting to develop their capabilities as managers. You might think that there isn't anything very new in that. In one way you would be right. The fact that very many people want to learn to become better managers is not new, and for many years a wide range of approaches to such learning and development has been available. These have included courses leading to formal qualifications, organizationally based management development programmes and a whole variety of self-study materials. A copious literature, extending from academic textbooks to sometimes idiosyncratic prescriptions from successful managers and consultants, has existed to aid – or perhaps confuse – the potential seeker after managerial truth and enlightenment.

So what is new about this series? In fact, a great deal – marking in some ways a revolution in our thinking both about the art of managing and also the process of developing managers.

Where did it all begin? Like most revolutions, although there may be a single, identifiable act that precipitated the uprising, the roots of discontent are many and long established. The debate about the performance of British managers, the way managers are educated and trained, and the extent to which shortcomings in both these areas have contributed to our economic decline, has been running for several decades.

Until recently, this debate had been marked by periods of frenetic activity – stimulated by some report or enquiry and perhaps ending in some new initiatives or policy changes – followed by relatively long periods of comparative calm. But the underlying causes for concern persisted. Basically, the majority of managers in the UK appeared to have little or no training for their role, certainly far less than their counterparts in our major competitor nations. And there was concern about the nature, style and appropriateness of the management education and training that was available.

The catalyst for this latest revolution came in late 1986 and early 1987, when three major reports reopened the whole issue. The 1987 reports were *The Making of British Managers* by John Constable and Roger McCormick, carried out for the British Institute of Management and the CBI, and *The Making of Managers* by Charles Handy, carried out for the (then) Manpower Services Commission, National Economic Development Office and British Institute of Management. The 1986 report, which often receives less recognition than it deserves as a key contribution to the recent changes, was *Management Training: context and process* by Iain Mangham and Mick Silver, carried out for the

Economic and Social Research Council and the Department of Trade and Industry.

It is not the place to review in detail what the reports said. Indeed, they and their consequences are discussed in several places in this series of books. But essentially they confirmed that:

- British managers were undertrained by comparison with their counterparts internationally.
- The majority of employers invested far too little in training and developing their managers.
- Many employers found it difficult to specify with any degree of detail just what it was that they required successful managers to be able to do.

The Constable/McCormick and Handy reports advanced various recommendations for addressing these problems, involving an expansion of management education and development, a reformed structure of qualifications and a commitment from employers to a code of practice for management development. While this analysis was not new, and had echoes of much that had been said in earlier debates, this time a few leading individuals determined that the response should be both radical and permanent. The response was coordinated by the newly established Council for Management Education and Development (now the National Forum for Management Education and Development (NFMED)) under the energetic and visionary leadership of Bob (now Sir Bob) Reid of Shell UK (now chairman of the British Railways Board).

Under the umbrella of NFMED a series of employer-led working parties tackled the problem of defining what it was that managers should be able to do, and how this differed for people at different levels in their organizations; how this satisfactory ability to perform might be verified; and how an appropriate structure of management qualifications could be put in place. This work drew upon the methods used to specify vocational standards in industry and commerce, and led to the development and introduction of competence-based management standards and qualifications. In this context, competence is defined as the ability to perform the activities within an occupation or function to the standards expected in employment.

It is this competence-based approach that is new in our thinking about the manager's capabilities. It is also what is new about this series of books, in that they are designed to support both this new structure of management standards, and of development activities based on it. The series was originally commissioned to support the Institute of Management's Certificate and Diploma qualifications, which were one of the first to be based on the new standards. However, these books are equally appropriate to any university, college or indeed company course leading to a certificate in management or diploma in management studies.

The standards were specified through an extensive process of consultation with a large number of managers in organizations of many different types and sizes. They are therefore employment based and employer supported. And they fill the gap that Mangham and Silver identified – now we do have a language to describe what it is employers want their managers to be able to do – at least in part.

If you are engaged in any form of management development leading to a certificate or diploma qualification conforming to the national management standards, then you are probably already familiar with most of the key ideas on which the standards are based. To achieve their key purpose, which is defined as achieving the organization's objectives and continuously improving its performance, managers need to perform four key roles: managing operations, managing finance, managing people and managing information. Each of these key roles has a sub-structure of units and elements, each with associated performance and assessment criteria.

The reason for the qualification 'in part' is that organizations are different, and jobs within them are different. Thus the generic management standards probably do not cover all the management competences that you may need to possess in your job. There are almost certainly additional things, specific to your own situation in your own organization, that you need to be able to do. The standards are necessary, but almost certainly not sufficient. Only you, in discussion with your boss, will be able to decide what other capabilities you need to possess. But the standards are a place to start, a basis on which to build. Once you have demonstrated your proficiency against the standards, it will stand you in good stead as you progress through your organization, or change jobs.

So how do the new standards change the process by which you develop yourself as a manager? They change the process of development, or of gaining a management qualification, quite a lot. It is no longer a question of acquiring information and facts, perhaps by being 'taught' in some classroom environment, and then being tested to see what you can recall. It involves demonstrating, in a quite specific way, that you can do certain things to a particular standard of performance. And because of this, it puts a much greater onus on you to manage your own development, to decide how you can demonstrate any particular competence, what evidence you need to present, and how you can collect it. Of course, there will always be people to advise and guide you in this, if you need help.

But there is another dimension, and it is to this that this series of books is addressed. While the standards stress ability to perform, they do not ignore the traditional knowledge base that has been associated with 'management studies'. Rather, they set this in a different context. The standards are supported by 'underpinning knowledge and understanding' which has three components:

- Purpose and context, which is knowledge and understanding of the manager's objectives, and of the relevant organizational and environmental influences, opportunities and values.
- Principles and methods, which is knowledge and understanding of the theories, models, principles, methods and techniques that provide the basis of competent managerial performance.
- Data, which is knowledge and understanding of specific facts likely to be important to meeting the standards.

Possession of the relevant knowledge and understanding underpinning the standards is needed to support competent managerial performance as specified in the standards. It also has an important role in supporting the transferability of management capabilities. It helps to ensure that you have done more than learned 'the way we do things around here' in your own organization. It indicates a recognition of the wider things which underpin competence, and that you will be able to change jobs or organizations and still be able to perform effectively.

These books cover the relevant knowledge and understanding underpinning the management standards, most specifically in the category of principles and methods. But their coverage is not limited to the minimum required by the standards, and extends in both depth and breadth in many areas. The authors have tried to approach these underlying principles and methods in a practical way. They use many short cases and examples which we hope will demonstrate how, in practice, the principles and methods, and knowledge of purpose and context plus data, support the ability to perform as required by the management standards. In particular we hope that this type of presentation will enable you to identify and learn from similar examples in your own managerial work.

You will already have noticed that one consequence of this new focus on the standards is that the traditional 'functional' packages of knowledge and theory do not appear. The standard textbook titles such as 'quantitative methods', 'production management', 'organizational behaviour', etc. disappear. Instead, principles and methods have been collected together in clusters that more closely match the key roles within the standards. You will also find a small degree of overlap in some of the volumes, because some principles and methods support several of the individual units within the standards. We hope you will find this useful reinforcement.

Having described the positive aspects of standards-based management development, it would be wrong to finish without a few cautionary remarks. The developments described above may seem simple, logical and uncontroversial. It did not always seem that way in the years of work which led up to the introduction of the standards. To revert to the revolution analogy, the process has been marked by ideological conflict and battles over sovereignty and territory. It has sometimes been unclear which side various parties are on – and indeed how many sides there are! The revolution, if well advanced, is not at an end. Guerrilla warfare continues in parts of the territory.

Perhaps the best way of describing this is to say that, while competence-based standards are widely recognized as at least a major part of the answer to improving managerial performance, they are not the whole answer. There is still some debate about the way competences are defined, and whether those in the standards are the most appropriate on which to base assessment of managerial performance. There are other models of management competences than those in the standards.

There is also a danger in separating management performance into a set of discrete components. The whole is, and needs to be, more than the sum of the parts. Just like bowling an off-break in cricket, practising a golf swing or forehand drive in tennis, you have to combine all the separate movements into a smooth, flowing action. How you combine the competences, and build on them, will mark your own individual style as a manager.

We should also be careful not to see the standards as set in stone. They determine what today's managers need to be able to do. As the arena in which managers operate changes, then so will the standards. The lesson for all of us as managers is that we need to go on learning and developing, acquiring new skills or refining existing ones. Obtaining your certificate or diploma is like passing a mile post, not crossing the finishing line.

All the changes and developments of recent years have brought management qualifications, and the processes by which they are gained, much closer to your job as a manager. We hope these books support this process by providing bridges between your own experience and the underlying principles and methods which will help you to demonstrate your competence. Already, there is a lot of evidence that managers enjoy the challenge of demonstrating competence, and find immediate benefits in their jobs from the programmes based on these new-style qualifications. We hope you do too. Good luck in your career development.

Paul Jervis

Preface

It is more than twenty years since Peter Drucker[1] said something remarkably simple which set marketing in a new and exciting context:

> There will always, one can assume, be need for some selling. But the aim of marketing is to make selling superfluous. The aim of marketing is to know and understand the customer so well that the product or service fits him and sells itself. Ideally, marketing should result in a customer who is ready to buy. All that should be needed then is to make the product or service available . . .

Since then, marketing has repeatedly come back to that idea of the customer as the key to the marketer's success. The whole business and management world is focusing more and more on the customer as a key to an organization's and to each individual manager's success.

One of the ideas which has helped the customer to become so important in management terms is the recognition that markets exist within, as well as outside, organizations. This has broadened our understanding of the marketing function in new ways which intrude on general management and human resource management fields. It has also made it clear that other management functions directly affect the organization's marketing in subtle and complex ways which need to be appreciated and understood by all managers.

Marketing goes beyond departmental or functional boundaries and is a general management issue – and the growth of interest in the internal market and in concepts such as Total Quality Management have confirmed this. Now we see a much stronger emphasis on customer needs and quality of service in every area of management. There is a growing realization that marketing is not simply a management function or set of processes. It is a core element of management philosophy.

This book is intended to challenge your understanding of your function within your own organization, which I believe to be a proper objective of any business textbook. In addition, I believe that it is very important that we should all adopt a more customer-oriented approach to all of our operational and other managerial skills. This is extremely important to all readers who wish to prepare themselves for a Level One Management qualification. It is also important to realize that such skills and such a perspective will also prepare you for your studies on Level Two Management courses.

I personally believe that any manager at any level in any organization will possess a strong competitive advantage if he or she has a clear and dynamic view of his or her customers. Such a person will win budgets, win support and implement plans which have an excellent chance of succeeding. The result is not simply a more successful organization but a more successful manager.

However, it is very easy to understand ideas which are logical and appealing but it can be hard work putting them into practice. This book is intended to help you by creating the foundations upon which your success can be built. You will discover that the approach in this book is not for the exclusive use of budding marketing professionals. You will be able to use the approach and skills taught here in your own management situation and take them with you as you progress up your chosen career path.

I would like to finish this preface with a quotation from Adam Smith's *The Wealth of Nations*.[2]

> Consumption is the sole end and purpose of all production and the interests of the product ought to be attended to, only so far as it may be necessary for promoting those of the consumer.

In a world which was possibly simpler than today's, he had the opportunity to discover a truth which we must all bear in mind. We need our customers!

References

1 Drucker, Peter F. (1974) *Management, Tasks, Responsibilities, Practices*, William Heinemann Ltd, London, p. 64.
2 Smith, Adam (1937) *The Wealth of Nations*, Random House, New York.

Ian Smith

1 The context

The marketing point of view

I have a dream about the future of Safeway. One day we shall have 500 stores, each perfectly adapted to the needs of the community it serves; we shall sell 20,000 products of which a third will be Safeway own brand; these own brands will match or beat the quality of the leading proprietary brands; we shall trade seven days a week and every minute that we are open, we shall fully satisfy every customer.

We shall be known and loved by every consumer; known and respected by every supplier; known and admired by every financial institution; known and valued by every member of government; known and understood by every journalist.

We are, I judge, about 60 per cent of the way towards my dream. Our marketing reflects both where we are and where we want to be. I apply a marketing point of view to pretty well everything we do and I work at making the idea of marketing pervasive throughout the business.

Sir Alastair Grant, Chairman & Chief Executive, Argyll Group Plc

This mission statement sets the direction for everyone in the business. It shows that every manager and every employee is concerned with meeting customer needs, all of the time, whatever they do. 'Customers', in many ways, includes suppliers, journalists, members of government as well as consumers. The customer tells us 'where we are and where we want to be'; so in managing and planning the future we must always keep the customer in mind. 'We shall have 500 stores, each perfectly adapted to the needs of the community it serves'; we need to be flexible in our approach to our customers and not impose rigid policies which suit our internal requirements. 'Every minute that we are open, we shall fully satisfy every customer'; that is the ultimate challenge to every manager. It is the reason why the customer must be the focus for every manager.

Why bother with customers?

In the Preface, I quoted Adam Smith as saying that the purpose of production is consumption and that, if you serve your customers' interests, you will also be serving your own. This not only applies to manufacturing organizations, but also to the service and non-profit sectors, as well as to the exchange of goods and services within organizations.

Figure 1.1 shows:

■ Customers exist inside and outside organizations.
■ Internal customers may also be external customers.

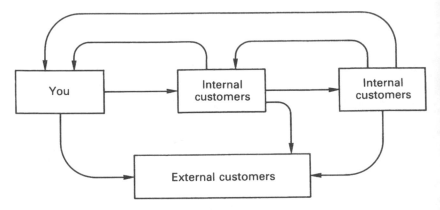

Figure 1.1 *Simplified map of flows to the internal and external customer*

■ Relations with internal customers affect the final service or product received by external customers.

Once you have identified who your customers are, you will be able to answer the question 'why bother with customers?' for yourself.

Figure 1.1 indicates the existence of an internal market, and there are several types of internal market. You already have relations with a number of internal customers and you know that you need to keep those customers satisfied in order to operate effectively. Your link with the external customers may be twice or three times removed, but you will be able to trace the effect of your work on the final quality of goods or services delivered to external customers. You will also be able to see the value which you add to the final product or service and you will be able to see how the quality of those internal relations affects relations with external customers.

Before outlining the remaining chapters, I would like you to consider the cartoon in Figure 1.2.

New ideas do not often fit within our existing belief structures. Hence the quote that 'if God had intended that we should be able to fly He would have given us wings'. This cartoon is an allegory for Western management in the past. A belief in our manufacturing supremacy and market dominance ensured that we did not notice our decline until it was almost too late, and it still took us a long time to learn from the competitors who succeeded us. Are you an ostrich, too, or are you prepared to allow yourself to see things in a new way – a way which might challenge your old view and the view shared by your colleagues?

Scope of the book

At its most basic level, this book deals with the management of operations and marketing. At another level it deals with the concepts,

Figure 1.2 *Ostriches. Source: Clark, Mary E.,* Ariadne's Thread – the Search for New Modes of Thinking, *Macmillan, 1989*

skills and processes which relate to these areas of management. It addresses the basic philosophy which drives these elements and justifies them emotionally as well as intellectually and practically. There is also a general model to work from in the form of the MCI competences, and I will refer to the operational standards prescribed by MCI throughout the text. This will be primarily at Management Level One, but I will also cover relevant standards at Management Level Two. Finally, this book addresses the needs of a very broad range of managers in an extensive range of sectors of the economy. It should be relevant to you and you should be able to use all of what is being covered here at different stages of your management career.

The chapters and the competences

The book is divided into three important aspects of meeting customer needs:

1 Who are the customers?
2 Interactions with customers.
3 Managing the processes.

The first part of the book focuses on the customers – who they are, how to identify and understand them, and how to listen to them.

Chapter 2 looks at identifying and describing individual customers and their buying behaviour.

Chapter 3 looks at segmenting and organizing your understanding of customers to consider them as markets.

Chapter 4 deals with how we listen to our customers.

The middle part of the book deals with the basic interactions between us and our customers.

Chapter 5 looks at what we provide and what that means to our customers and to ourselves.

Chapter 6 looks at pricing and values: the exchanges inherent in any provision or transaction.

Chapter 7 deals with the two perspectives which are central to any customer/supplier interactions. It looks at the manager as customer and deals with managing supply, it then looks at how we deliver our products or services.

Chapter 8 looks at the communications between ourselves and our customers.

The final part of the book looks at how we manage the processes in more detail.

Chapter 9 looks at the management of our operations and how we need to manage the inputs and outputs in our department to meet customer needs most effectively.

Chapter 10 focuses on quality and how to manage that element within the context of meeting customer needs.

Chapter 11 deals with customer satisfaction and complaints and looks at how this needs to be controlled and managed.

Chapter 12 deals with planning and with managing the planning processes.

2 Who are your customers?

Why this chapter is important

Before we can meet customer needs, we have to understand who our customers are and what influences them when they are buying. This chapter outlines the techniques used by marketing professionals to research and analyse customer needs and identify buying factors. You can apply these techniques to your own activities, even if you are not dealing with external customers. You will also gain an understanding of why you are asked to carry out some of your operations in a specific way to meet the needs of external customers.

What is a customer?

A customer is an individual or group of individuals to whom you provide one or more products or services. You may receive goods or services in return or be paid through a third party who may also be your customer. These exchanges form a series of links in a chain which joins with other chains and drives not only organizations but industries and economies.

In purely economic terms, each transaction must contain benefits to each party, i.e. a price which is acceptable to the customer and which provides you with sufficient rewards (or profits) to induce you to continue with the enterprise.

In the non-profit or voluntary sectors, in other sectors such as public services and in internal markets, profit may not be definable in monetary terms. However, there must still be a satisfactory balance of benefits for both parties.

For example, imagine a charity working to provide famine relief. You are moved by television reports of the famine and you pledge fifty pounds by phone using your credit card. This money is transferred to the charity's account and used to buy grain and ship it out for distribution in the stricken area. This is the possible chain of customers and suppliers which links your donation to that charity:

- The TV reporter.
- The company which employs the reporter.
- The different TV companies which used his report in their news coverage.
- The charity which helped him make the reports in exchange for exposure and promotion.
- The viewers who were moved and informed.

- The company which handles the telephone pledges.
- The banks and other financial institutions which handle the financial transactions.
- The companies and organizations which provide the food, transport and distribution.
- The government whose own relief efforts can be reduced or restricted while private individuals and organizations take on the main burden of relief.
- The people requiring help.

These are just some of the links in the chain and each customer may receive a number of rewards from different sources and may, in turn, satisfy part of the needs of each of their customers. What do you think you would get out of such a contribution and whose needs would you be satisfying?

In your own job you will already have worked out most of your customers and will be thinking that you have some clear idea of their motivations. Before you continue reading this book, jot down in your notebook the following column headings:

- My customers.
- What I provide.
- What I receive as a result.
- Who I receive it from.

Now write in the name of each of your customers, listing the other items against each customer. After doing this, consider who you may have missed out. It may be obvious to some of you that YOU might be YOUR OWN customer, especially if your primary source of job satisfaction is doing the job well and if you rely very little on others to assist. Return to your list and consider whether there might not be other additions.

When you feel that you have completed your list of customers and associated details, consider each column in turn, ask yourself the following questions and indicate your choices.

In the 'My customers' column, identify:

- Which customer is most important to you.
- Which is the most important customer as far as your boss is concerned.
- Which is the most important to your company as a whole.
- Which of your customers prizes your products or services the most.

In the 'What I provide' column, try to identify the provision which is most important to:

- You.
- Your boss.
- Your organization as a whole.
- Your customers.

In the 'What I receive as a result' and the 'Who I receive it from' columns carry out a similar exercise.

If you only have internal customers you may find it a strange exercise to carry out at first, but when you put some effort into it you will find that it helps you understand a number of things about your job and the workings of your department.

Complete this exercise by identifying a customer on your list who has direct contact with external customers and list the things which you do which enable that person or department to serve that external customer or customer group well. Can you identify improvements which you could make in your service which would result in an improved service to that external customer? This exercise will help you understand why you should bother with customers, because as Kenichi Ohmae[1] says:

> In a free competitive economic world, there will be no stability in a corporation's performance if it allows its attention to be diverted from the basic business mission of serving customers. If it consistently succeeds in serving customers more effectively than its competitors, profit will follow.

What do we know about customers?

The most effective way of understanding and responding to your customers' needs is to put yourself in their position and try to understand why they choose to be your customers. Of course, in internal markets customers may not have a choice, so we will start with individuals and groups who do.

We can identify differences between customers in consumer markets and industrial or business markets:

- Customers in the consumer market will tend to be individuals or small family groups buying for themselves.
- Customers in the industrial or business market will be acting on behalf of an organization.

The motivations and considerations which lie behind buying decisions will be profoundly affected by these factors.

Consumer markets

We have some unique insight into customers in this area as we are all consumers ourselves. However, trying to make general statements about our own buying behaviour, before we try to extend them to others, is extremely difficult. Furthermore, we may not be able to tell why we bought a particular product or service even a short time after we made the purchase. We have to acknowledge that each purchasing decision that a customer makes will be influenced by a wide range of factors.

Factors affecting customer decisions in consumer markets

Every consumer is influenced by factors which change and vary in importance throughout their lives. In consumer markets, these are the most important factors to consider when you try to understand the buying motives of your customers and markets:

- Gender.
- Age.
- Marital status.
- Children in household.
- Income.
- Socio-economic groups.
- Occupation.
- Personal financial management.
- Home ownership.
- Location.
- Combinations of factors.
- Life cycle/Sagacity.
- Geo-demographic systems.
- Culture.
- Lifestyle/psychographics.
- Psychology.

Gender

Certain consumer products and services appear to be aimed at one or the other sex, for example, clothes or specialist healthcare products. However, in reality, there are very few products or services which are not bought by both sexes. Confusion increases where the purchaser or end user is not the sole decision maker.

Age

A consumer's age may provide some clues to their lifestyle and their interests, and products or services can be specifically targeted at an age group, for example, retirement homes, Club 18 to 30 or the Puffin book range. Age can be summarized in ranges, unlike gender. Often the age ranges are in decades starting at fifteen years old:

15–18, 18–20, 21–25, 25–34, 35–44, 45–54, 55–64, 65+.

Marital status

Marital status is a significant factor when it is combined with other factors such as children and income and where a product or service is designed specifically for people of a given marital status. However, there are many products and services which are aimed at married couples or single people for image or other reasons. Hence the use of the stable family unit in many food and household product adverts, and the use of prosperous young single people or couples in adverts for what are essentially small family cars. The sub-divisions, or breaks as they are sometimes known, usually include the following:

Single, Married, Divorced/Separated, Widowed.

Children in household

The presence of children in a household can be a significant factor affecting the disposable income of the household, its lifestyle and attitudes and its consumption pattern. There is a vast difference in disposable income and lifestyle between two-income families with children and two-income families without children. The age of the children also affects disposable income.

Income

Not everyone is prepared to give a researcher truthful or accurate answers about their income, so respondents are asked to state their income range in either £5000 or £10 000 breaks. For ease of control and use, ranges tend to be in £10 000 breaks, but lower income ranges are broken into smaller amounts to take into account the significance of an increase in incomes at the lower end of the scale:

Up to £5000, £5000–7500, £7500–10 000, £10 000–12 500, £12 500–15 000, £15 000–25 000, £25 000–35 000, £35 000–45 000, £45 000–55 000, £55 000–65 000, over £65 000.

Income is described in two ways – net or gross. Net income is after tax and any other basic living costs have been deducted, whereas gross income is total income before tax and deductions.

Socio-economic groups

The socio-economic groups most commonly used in the UK were developed as a rationalization of social class in the 1950s. However, they are severely flawed both in their structure and in their value as a model of today's society. In 1981, the Market Research Society published an evaluation of social grades which covers five socio-economic or social class groupings: A, B, C1, C2, D and E.

A   Higher managerial, administrative or professional.
B   Intermediate managerial, administrative or professional.
C1 Supervisory, clerical, junior administrative or professional.
C2 Skilled manual workers.
D   Semi-skilled and unskilled manual workers.
E   State pensioners, widows, casual and lowest grade earners.

As a factor influencing purchasing or buying behaviour it is being superseded by more up-to-date forms of classification focused on the Head of Household or Chief Wage Earner. In the most stringent surveys the researcher will ask a series of screening questions related to the person's occupation, status at work, number of people they supervise, size of employing organization, rank or grade and qualifications before classifying by social grade.

Occupation

Occupation is often too complex to help us discern its value as a factor in buying behaviour in general consumer markets. In fact, there are few pieces of research work where the actual occupation is recorded apart from the National Readership Survey. If occupation is recorded it tends to be in categories almost identical to those describing socio-economic group. However, most occupation groupings also include some information on the type of sector in which the respondent is employed, for example, the teaching profession, civil service, engineering, or the professions.

Personal financial management

A consumer's use of credit, financial management ability and approach to money generally can be useful factors in evaluating their buying behaviour. Ownership and use of credit cards, numbers and types of bank and building society accounts are not simply indicators of financial well-being, but can prove to be indicators of a person's approach to buying and may have a bearing on their willingness or ability to buy specific products or services.

Home ownership

Home ownership results in specific needs and responsibilities which correlate directly with their purchasing patterns. There has been a major shift in home ownership in recent years and, despite the recession, many more people own their home today than at the beginning of the 1980s.

Location

Where a consumer lives may have an important bearing on buying behaviour. Certain products or services may be limited to specific locations and there are cultural and economic factors which predominate in different regions. Thus, rural and urban consumers differ in a number of ways, as may inner city, council estate and suburban dwellers.

Combinations of factors

We can increase our understanding of buying behaviour when we combine various factors together, for example, the effect of children on the disposable income of a family. This suggests that although income may be useful as a buying factor, it is more powerful when you can establish the level of disposable income in a household. Combining income with home ownership, partner's status and number and ages of children is one way of doing this. Other obvious combinations are age and sex, socio-economic group and sex and so on. These simple combinations will affect not only our understanding of buying, but help us gain a greater understanding of particular purchasers or customers. Using the types of information above, we can create more sophisticated descriptions of people and their buying potential.

Life cycle/Sagacity

Many of the buying factors come together to create an environment where certain types of behaviour may predominate. Using the basic demographic data, for example, it is possible to put together a general model of the different stages of a person's life. One such model was created by William D. Wells and George Gubar[2] in America during the 1960s. They identified nine stages in what they called the family life cycle. These were:

1 Bachelor stage: young, single people not living at home.
2 Newly married couples: young, no children.
3 Full nest I: youngest child under six.
4 Full nest II: youngest child six or over.
5 Full nest III: older married couples with dependent children.
6 Empty nest I: older married couples, no children at home.
7 Empty nest II: older married couples, retired, no children at home.
8 Solitary survivor: in labour force.
9 Solitary survivor: retired.

Although the concept is a good one, it does not address the true variety of modern society. It assumes a 'normal family life' and ignores the variety of normal family lifestyles which includes single parent families, divorced or unmarried single people living on their own or sharing a house or flat, families with three generations living together, or mature single people living with and caring for elderly relatives.

The other drawback to such systems is their applicability. Sagacity, developed by the research company RSL Ltd, uses the huge data sets available from the National Readership Survey (NRS), but the

The basic thesis of the Sagacity grouping is that people have different aspirations and behaviour patterns as they go through their life cycle. Four main stages of life cycle are defined which are sub-divided by income and occupation groups:

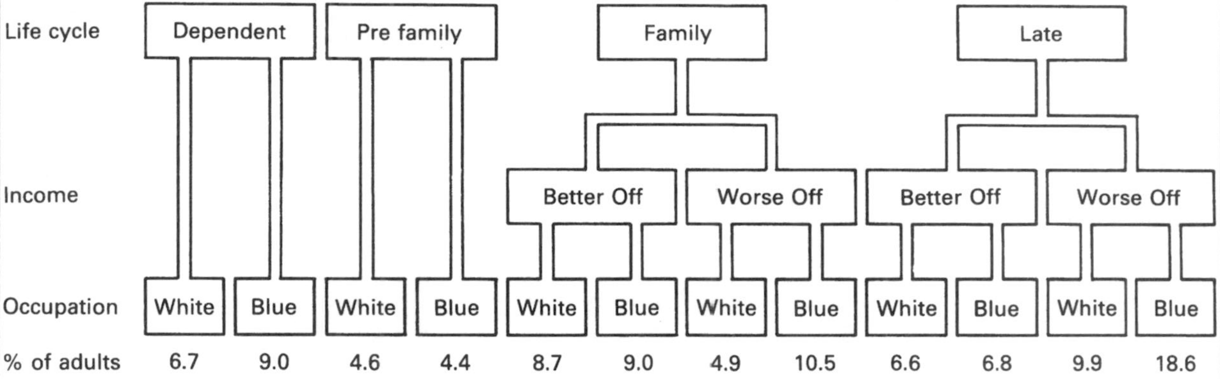

Life cycle	Dependent		Pre family		Family				Late			
Income					Better Off		Worse Off		Better Off		Worse Off	
Occupation	White	Blue	White	Blue	White	Blue	White	Blue	White	Blue	White	Blue
% of adults	6.7	9.0	4.6	4.4	8.7	9.0	4.9	10.5	6.6	6.8	9.9	18.6

Definitions of life cycle stages
Dependent – Mainly under 24s, living at home or full-time student.
Pre-family – Under 35s, who have established their own household but have no children.
Family – Housewives and heads of household, under 65, with one or more children in the household.
Late – Includes all adults whose children have left home or who are over 35 and childless.

Definitions of occupation groups
White – Head of household is in the ABC1 occupation group.
Blue – Head of household is in the C2DE occupation group.

Source: Research Services Ltd, year to June 1989.

Figure 2.1 *The Sagacity life cycle groupings*

definition of and consequent classification of individuals according to the Sagacity model (see Figure 2.1) requires very good data on a very wide range of demographic factors for each respondent and needs a considerable amount of computer power. It is therefore not so easy to replicate Sagacity in basic market research.

Geo-demographic systems

The geo-demographic classification system classifies groups of people according to where they live and according to a wide range of demographic, socio-economic and housing data which are available on small areas. The ACORN system (A Classification Of Residential Neighbourhoods) was created by identifying different variables which could be obtained from the census at enumeration district level – small areas which contain approximately 150 households. This data gives us, for example, the percentage of the population of each enumeration district in each of the different breaks in the age range, the percentage of men and women to be found in each of the enumeration districts, the percentage of homes with inside and outside toilets in each district, and many other factors.

Computer programs were developed to assess forty such variables, compare each enumeration district with the others, and group all of the most similar districts together in clusters. The process is actually very complex and has a number of technical difficulties, but it provides a meaningful range of neighbourhood types (see Figure 2.2).

Since the initial classification, vast amounts of research have been carried out on these area types and market researchers have used these classifications to help them structure samples and sampling systems. Geo-demographic systems tend to be effective discriminators of purchasing behaviour, allowing marketers to gain a greater understanding of the groups of people who buy specific products or services. It has also been possible to refine the classifications further and allocate the area types to areas as small as postal codes which contain approximately fifteen to twenty homes.

Culture

Cultural influences can affect buying behaviour in a number of ways. In the UK we have a number of regional and racial cultural variations which influence purchase decisions. These influences can be very subtle and there have been many studies carried out to try and understand the role of culture. Within each culture smaller groups exist, known as sub-cultures, with their own distinctive values. Within cultures and sub-cultures there are strong forces which encourage each member to conform or aspire to the values of their 'reference group'. These groups can exert 'peer' pressure which can influence individual members to change or modify their behaviour in terms of their needs, aspirations, wants and even purchasing patterns.

ACORN stands for 'A Classification Of Residential Neighbourhoods'. The system was developed by CACI. The table below shows ACORN's 38 neighbourhood types, the 11 groups they form, and their share of the GB population of 54 086 798 in 1987. ACORN is based on the Government's Census of Great Britain conducted in 1981. The 1987 populations of the 1981 census neighbourhoods are derived from CACI's proprietary demographic model of Great Britain.

ACORN types		% of 1987 population	ACORN groups	
A 1	Agricultural villages	2.6	3.5 Agricultural areas	A
A 2	Areas of farms and smallholdings	0.8		
B 3	Post-war functional private housing	4.3		
B 4	Modern private housing, young families	3.5	Modern family	
B 5	Established private family housing	5.9	17.1 housing, higher	B
B 6	New detached houses, young families	2.8	incomes	
B 7	Military bases	0.6		
C 8	Mixed owner-occupied and council estates	3.5		
C 9	Small town centres and flats above shops	4.1	Older housing of	
C10	Villages with non-farm employment	4.8	17.8 intermediate	C
C11	Older private housing, skilled workers	5.5	status	
D12	Unmodernized terraces, older people	2.5		
D13	Older terraces, lower income families	1.4	4.3 Older terraced	D
D14	Tenement flats lacking amenities	0.4	housing	
E15	Council estates, well-off older workers	3.5		
E16	Recent council estates	2.8	Council estates –	
E17	Better council estates, younger workers	4.9	13.0 category I	E
E18	Small council houses, often Scottish	1.9		
F 19	Low rise estates in industrial towns	4.6		
F 20	Inter-war council estates, older people	2.9	9.0 Council estates –	F
F 21	Council housing, elderly people	1.4	category II	
G22	New council estates in inner cities	2.0		
G23	Overspill estates, higher unemployment	3.0	7.2 Council estates –	G
G24	Council estates with some overcrowding	1.5	category III	
G25	Council estates with greatest hardship	0.6		
H26	Multi-occupied older housing	0.4		
H27	Cosmopolitan owner-occupied terraces	1.1	Mixed inner	
H28	Multi-let housing in cosmopolitan areas	0.7	3.8 metropolitan	H
H29	Better-off cosmopolitan areas	1.7	areas	
I 30	High status non-family areas	2.1		
I 31	Multi-let big old houses and flats	1.5	4.2 High status non-	I
I 32	Furnished flats, mostly single people	0.5	family areas	
J 33	Inter-war semis, white collar workers	5.7		
J 34	Spacious inter-war semis, big gardens	5.0	Affluent	
J 35	Villages with wealthy older communities	2.9	15.9 suburban	J
J 36	Detached houses, exclusive suburbs	2.3	housing	
K37	Private houses, well-off older residents	2.3	3.8 Better-off	K
K38	Private flats, older single people	1.6	retirement areas	
U39	Unclassified	0.5	0.5 Unclassified	U
		100.0		

Figure 2.2 *ACORN profile of Great Britain. Source: CACI Market Analysis 1989,* © CACI

It may not be possible to carry out major measurable research to ascertain the effects of peer pressure. Advertising which utilizes peer pressure will be created not as a result of detailed research but through personal understanding or empathy with the target group. Qualitative research, which is covered later, can shed some light on this area and is used extensively by advertisers and marketers who wish to understand aspects of peer pressure or other cultural issues.

Lifestyle/psychographics

As Philip Kotler[3] points out, 'Lifestyle attempts to profile a person's way of being and acting in the world.' There are two main approaches to lifestyle classification. One uses a long questionnaire broken down into four main topics:

1 Activities (such as hobbies, clubs, entertainment).
2 Interests (such as home, food, fashion).
3 Opinions (on such topics as politics, economics, education).
4 Basic demographic information about each respondent.

In the questionnaire, the respondent has to say whether he or she strongly agrees, agrees, disagrees or strongly disagrees with a series of statements. These responses are analysed on the computer to identify clusters of people with similar lifestyles. When combined with demographic data and analysed against purchasing data, these lifestyle groups can provide valuable insights into consumer motivations.

The research company BMRB has carried out a great deal of work in this area in the UK using lifestyle questionnaires which have been attached to their large consumer survey Target Group Index (TGI).

The second type of lifestyle classification, developed in the USA by Arnold Mitchell[4] of SRI International, is based on the same technique but approaches the classification from a psychological point of view. Mitchell explored the values of the individuals in each group and identified nine development stages that people appeared to go through. Each stage affected the person's attitudes, behaviour and psychological needs:

■ Need-driven stage;
 – survivors or sustainers;
■ Inner- or outer-directed stage;
 – I-am-me, experientials and societally conscious (inner);
 – belongers, emulators and achievers stages (outer);
■ Integrated stage (achieved by only a small percentage).

In the UK, the market research company Taylor Nelson has developed and successfully used a similar classification system. Systems like this are interesting but require a massive amount of research work. The importance of these systems lies in their recognition of the value of each individual's personal interests and

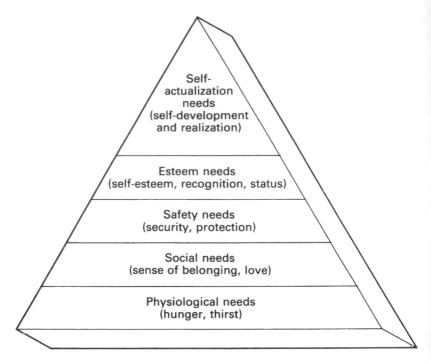

Figure 2.3 *Maslow's hierarchy of needs*

motivations as contributing to our understanding of groups of individuals. Unlike most demographic data, they attempt to describe people in less absolute and more dynamic terms.

Psychology

Abraham Maslow[5] identified a hierarchy of needs (see Figure 2.3) which suggests that needs are felt at different levels by everyone:

- Basic physiological need for survival.
- Need for protection and security.
- Social needs such as love, belonging.
- Esteem needs such as status or self-esteem.
- Self actualization needs which involve self-development.

Summary

What you know and understand about each of these factors will help you to maximize their value. When relating them to your own knowledge and experience, consider how you think of yourself and your friends, relations and associates. What are the most important factors for you and for your parents, close relatives and your partner? How might they affect your own and their purchases of groceries, a stereo system, a car or a washing machine?

Factors influencing industrial or business customers

In the previous section, we looked at factors which might affect our consumers' buying behaviour. Each factor related to the consumer as an individual. Now we must look at external customers who are not buying for themselves, but for an organization. In such cases, we must consider factors which go beyond the individual.

The customer's personal situation

Here are some of the things you may need to know about the person you deal with:

- Job title.
- Department name.
- The customer's status in the department.
- Scope of their authority.
- Who the product is for.
- Who decides what to buy.
- Who instructs them to buy.
- Who pays for it.
- Who will have to handle any after-sales problems.
- Who enjoys the success or suffers the failure

Factors related to the customer's department

The nature of your customer's department can help you understand your customer's buying behaviour.

- If your customer is the manager in charge of the department, what is the management style?
- If the customer is not the manager, understanding the management style will help you meet the needs of the customer and satisfy your customer's internal customers at the same time.
- If the department is buying for itself, the relationship will be different from the situation where the department buys for the whole of the organization.
- The size and importance of your customer's department within its organization may also have some bearing on how it acts as a customer.
- The cost of what you are selling may constitute a large or a small cost to your customer or their department.

These factors will influence your customer's view of you and will affect any customer expectations and needs.

Factors related to the customer's organization

The organization which employs your customer will influence their approach to you and your product or service. The factors included here are important, but not exhaustive.

Size Large organizations tend to have detailed formal buying procedures whereas smaller organizations are less formal and less rigid in their approach. Furthermore, there may be a wide range of people involved in purchasing decisions in larger organizations, but fewer people are likely to be involved in purchasing decisions in smaller companies. The criteria used to assess suppliers and 'approve' them may be comprehensive and very stringent in a large organization, while a smaller organization may use more basic criteria with different priorities.

Industry sectors We can make general sub-divisions such as service sector, industrial and manufacturing sector, the non-profit or voluntary sectors, education, or public services. Alternatively, you can sub-divide according to whether they are privately owned, a public limited company, a charity, nationalized, a local or national government organization, national or multi-national. Each of these factors can affect the environment, constraints expectations and needs of your customer and may significantly affect buying behaviour.

A software company which specializes in providing tailor-made accounting systems for the financial sector will have different purchasing criteria for their computers than a software company specializing in the aerospace manufacturing sector. The type of machines, operating systems and technical specifications will differ considerably and the type of after-sales service agreements, maintenance and upgrading contracts they will seek may also differ greatly.

Location Geography can also play its part. A company's location relative to you may be significant, as may its location in an Enterprise Zone, or in an Assisted Area. If its location is in a region with a strong identity or in another country or if its parent company is based in another country, there may be strong influences which will affect the customer's buying behaviour.

Factors affecting customer decisions in internal markets

Internal markets are extremely important to consider as their operation affects the way in which each of us adds value to what we provide. Through the internal market you participate in making your organization work, and emotional as well as financial rewards come from the good relations you have with colleagues.

In the following example, you will see that internal markets do exist and that what is exchanged is influenced by the way you deal with customers and suppliers. As manager of a marketing department, I had a number of internal customers, including the accounts department. The marketing department generated both costs and revenue which were handled by the accounts department. I put together a budget at the beginning of the year and then updated the figures with forecasts and actual figures to be used in both the financial and management accounts.

As my customer, the accounts department was provided with information of actual and expected transactions, I produced clear data and some analyses. I also added a short written report on our markets, our competitors and the impact of legislation. This background information helped the accounts department to understand our position and why I changed my forecasts and other figures. This data was well presented and was followed up by a telephone call.

I did this because it was my policy to give an added value to all of my customers internally as well as externally. In exchange for that quality service I was given a high level of service from the accounts department. My budgets encountered less problems than other departmental budgets and I spent less time sorting out small details. My external suppliers and customers were served better by our accounts department and when I wished to settle an account earlier than normal, the accounts department nearly always obliged without complaint. I was kept well informed of any changes to the accounting system and, most significantly, the marketing director's job was made that much easier with a potential ally in the form of the finance director.

Using this example, we can identify some of the factors that might affect a customer's 'buying behaviour' in an internal market:

- Our first task is to recognize that we have customers and identify who they are.
- We must determine whether we are dealing with an individual or group of individuals such as a department.
- If we are dealing with a group, we need to know who the key person or persons are who will define the needs and expectations of the group.
- Some of the factors which applied to external customers will also apply to internal customers. For example:
  - Age may be significant, helping you anticipate the customer's expectations of you.
  - Their position in their department and in the organization as a whole.
  - Your understanding of who your customer serves and how your service or product will help your customer deliver their ultimate product or service.

Can you identify an internal customer or supplier who could be influenced in a similar way by your own and your staff's actions?

External factors affecting customers

In a later chapter I will look at the external environment in more detail, but here I want briefly to review the external factors which affect your

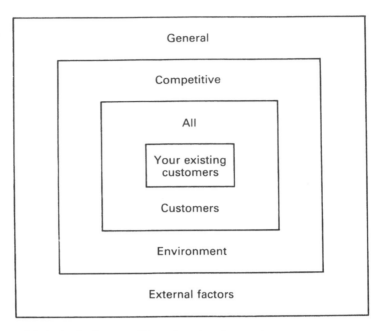

Figure 2.4 *A simple diagram of the external environment*

customers. Customers can be influenced in a number of ways summarized in Figure 2.4.

■ Influences present in your existing and past customer base.
■ Competitive influences.
■ Influences of the general external environment which can be summarized under the four headings:
  – Sociological.
  – Technological.
  – Economic.
  – Political.

These last four factors are known as the STEP Factors.

Sociological factors   Sociological factors aid our understanding of our customer's buying behaviour and help us predict behaviour or changes in behaviour in the future. For example, changes in society's attitude towards the environment have been reflected in a growing demand for environmentally friendly products and for changes in the way in which products are manufactured and used.

List the sociological factors which affect you and your customers.

Technological factors   Consumer expectations have been affected by the rapid developments in technology in the last twenty years and the rate of adoption of new technology appears to be increasing at a comparable rate to that of changes in technology. We now have the technology to make cars and other machines more economical while producing less pollution, and we are aware of environmental effects of pollution which could only be revealed to us by the latest technology. Thus we are being influenced and changed by the technological changes we experience, and this is being reflected in why, how and what we buy.

What technological factors do you think have affected both your own and your customers' attitudes, expectations and needs?

Economic factors Economic factors play a part in shaping our customers' expectations, needs, fears and attitudes. This in turn affects their decisions and their decision-making processes. Consumers and business customers will be affected by changes in interest rates, the exchange rate, the rate of inflation, recession and reflation, European monetary and fiscal policies, changes in the cost of crude oil or raw materials from the third world, and changes in the economies of important countries such as Germany, the USA and Japan.

List the factors which you think are most important to you and your customers.

Political factors Political change can affect us as consumers. The breakdown of the Soviet empire, the effect of German reunification and the opening up of Eastern Europe have seen investment shifted from the South to the East. Similarly, the effect of the Thatcher years on the UK has been significant with strong shifts in attitudes and expectations, in economic activity and in social behaviour. On a more mundane level, a report by the gas or electricity regulatory bodies can result in price changes or changes in customer service policy. Reports by the Monopolies and Mergers Commission can initiate or hinder changes in big corporations. Such reports can have profound effects on staff and their behaviour as customers.

List the political factors most important to you and your customers.

Buyer behaviour in the consumer sector

The process of making a decision and the influences which come to bear on that process have been studied by a number of people. Three approaches are described below:

1 The purchasing decision as a systematic process, a logical progression through definable stages which inevitably lead to the purchase.
2 The process of repeat purchase.
3 Sociological and psychological presentations of purchasing behaviour.

Purchasing as a systematic process

A great number of models have been designed to try to rationalize buyer behaviour in a comprehensive way which will allow you both to explain and to predict behaviour. They all involve a wide range of variables, and map out a system of interactions, causes and effects and logical flows from one stage to another. As tools to help us discuss and explore the issues, they are extremely useful but they all present considerable practical problems when applied.

The Howard and Sheth model

Howard and Sheth[6] developed a comprehensive model of brand choice over time (see Figure 2.5).

To summarize:

■ A customer is confronted with a stimulus at the input stage and his or her attention is caught.
■ The customer reacts to this stimulus and moves into the perceptual and learning constructs where information is processed, and he or she begins to form concepts of the brand based on, for example, motives, expectations and inhibitions.
■ External influences, based perhaps on the customer's perceptions of other brands, will also play a part in this process.
■ After purchase takes place, the customer can evaluate that purchase and predisposition towards the brand is modified resulting in changes in the output variables.

If you want to follow the process in more depth, here is a more detailed description. The model had four different components:

1 Input variables.
2 Hypothetical constraints.
3 Exogenous variables.
4 Output variables

1 **Input variables** These were split into three types:

– Significative stimuli: the elements of the brand itself which the purchaser will encounter (price, availability and distinctiveness).
– Symbolic stimuli: the symbolic representations of the brand found in advertising.
– Social stimuli: family type, social class and the family.

Between this set of variables and the output variables we find two components which attempt to map the processes of interaction, reaction and rationalization which result in the output component.

2 **Hypothetical constructs** These intervening variables are subdivided into two categories:

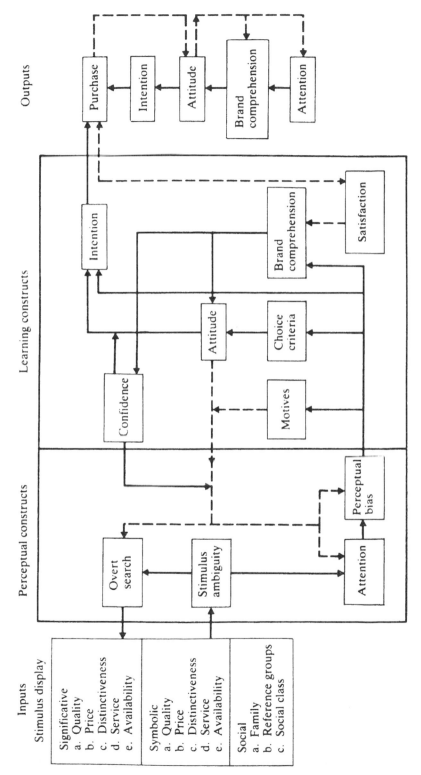

Figure 2.5 *The Howard–Sheth model of buyer behaviour. Source: J. N. Sheth and J. A. Howard, The Theory of Buyer Behaviour. John Wiley, 1969*

A The perceptual constructs – which deal with processing information and come in three forms:

1 The customer's sensitivity to information which involves the degree of control of flow of information;
2 The perceptual bias which is about the customer's distortion of or alteration of the information;
3 The search for information which deals with the customer's own search for information about brands and their characteristics.

B The learning constructs – which deal with the customer's formation of concepts which are sub-divided into six categories:

1 *Motive* which is self-explanatory;
2 *Brand potential of the evoked set* which means the customer's perception of how good a brand will be at satisfying its perceived goals;
3 *The decision mediators* which are the customer's own rules for matching and ranking competing brands;
4 *Predisposition* which is again self-explanatory;
5 *The inhibitors category* which covers environmental forces which make it difficult or impossible for the purchaser to buy his/her preferred brand;
6 *Satisfaction* which is a measure of actual experience against expectation.

3 **Exogenous variables** These are variables which can profoundly affect the buyer's decisions but, according to the authors, because the variables are external to the buyer, they are difficult to define very clearly and could consist of any of the other variables.

4 **Output variables** This group consists of five self-explanatory categories:

1 Attention.
2 Comprehension.
3 Attitude.
4 Intention.
5 Purchase behaviour.

This was one of the earliest models of its sort and, despite its difficult language and its imperfections, is still useful.

Other process models

The Engel–Kollat–Blackwell[7] model (Figure 2.6)
This model takes one of the aspects featured in the Howard–Sheth model and develops it further. Engel, Kollat and Blackwell concentrated on buyer behaviour as a decision-making process. They

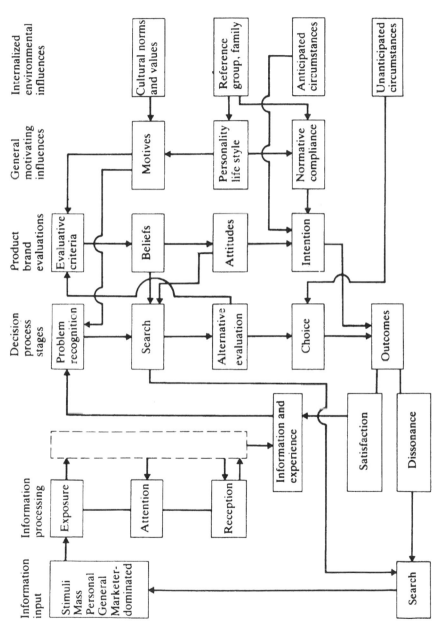

Figure 2.6 *The Engel–Kollat–Blackwell model. Source: J. Engel, D. Rollat and R. Blackwell, Consumer Behaviour, Dryden Press, 1978*

identified five stages in the decision-making process which are affected by a further five sets of variables. The five stages are:

1 Problem recognition: the customer is dissatisfied with the present brand.
2 Information search: customers seek out information from sources to which they are exposed.
3 Alternative evaluation: customers apply their beliefs and prejudices to all other brands.
4 Choice: this can be affected by other people or by changing circumstances, such as a drop in income or a change in priorities.
5 Outcome: post-purchase evaluation; the customer will feel satisfaction or doubt, perhaps feeling that another brand might have been a better choice.

The model assumes a conscious decision-making process and tries to describe it. The customer can move as rapidly or as slowly through the model as they need to and the routes through are flexible and easy to understand. However, the model still holds a number of variables which are either difficult to measure or whose importance or effect is unclear.

The Sheth family model (Figure 2.7)

The Sheth model[8] is intended to show how purchase decisions are made within the family, based on psychological systems for each member of the family. In the model Sheth identifies seven family and product factors which he claims will affect how the decision is made (in other words whether it is to be shared or individual decision). It shows us that social class is a strong determinant, with middle-class families being more likely to make joint purchasing decisions than their working-class counterparts. It also shows us that joint decisions are also prevalent when a high level of risk is attached to the purchase or, for example, in the choice of a holiday, when there is time to make the decision.

Such complex models are very attractive to academics but they are highly theoretical and extremely difficult (and enormously expensive) to test. Decision making is a hard process to explain but these models go some way towards explaining what might be involved.

Repeat purchasing models

Why do customers keep on buying the same brand? This phenomenon is known as brand loyalty. Philip Kotler[9] has described the process of repeat purchase in a simple five-stage model:

1 Problem recognition: recognition of need through internal recognition or through external influences such as advertising. By providing stimuli, you can help customers recognize and satisfy their needs.

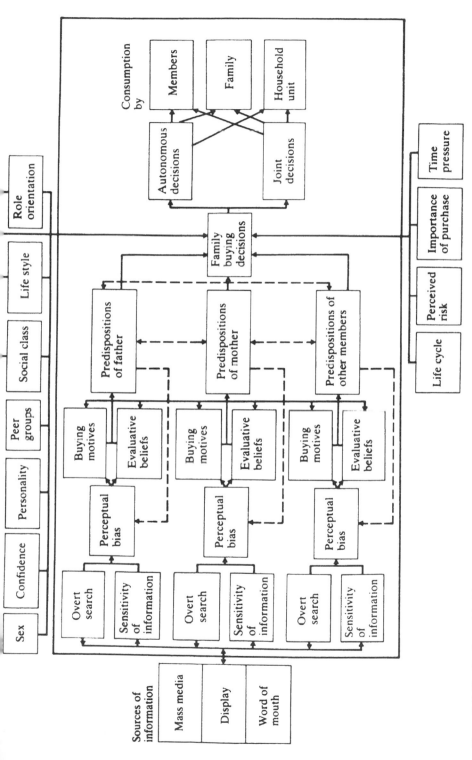

Figure 2.7 The Sheth model of family decision making. Source: 'A theory of family buying decisions' in Models of Buyer Behaviour, J. N. Sheth, Harper and Row, 1974, pp. 22–23

2 Information search: customers will be gathering information both consciously and subconsciously. You can provide customers with the right sort of information in the most appropriate way and at the most important and receptive time.

3 Evaluation of alternatives: Kotler identifies four filtering processes which help the individual to evaluate the alternatives:
   (a) Availability – no matter how committed a customer is to your products or services, if these are not in the shops or easily available, the customer will not buy them.
   (b) Awareness – if the customer does not know about your brand or product they will not seek it out and buy it.
   (c) Suitability – brands encompass an enormous amount of emotional and perceived characteristics which can become a barrier to purchase to the point where one cannot be substituted for another.
   (d) Customer choice – the customer buys what he or she has decided is best even though this may not appear logical to you.

4 Purchase decision: there are two ways of approaching this stage.
   (a) Brand framework – the customer has a framework of preferences and desired attributes for the product, evaluates each brand according to the mental framework, adjusts each evaluation according to the relative importance of each attribute or preference, and selects the brand with the best match of characteristics.
   (b) Brand positioning – the customer has a mental picture of the ideal brand and seeks the best substitute for the perfect brand.

5 Post-purchase behaviour: this is the key stage in understanding repeat purchase. Repeat purchase results from satisfaction; the customer experiencing dissatisfaction may try to return or abandon the product.

Organizational buying behaviour

There are a number of models in this area and much of what we have discussed so far can be used as input for these models.

The Sheth model of organizational buying

Sheth developed a model,[10] based on his earlier consumer version, which helps to highlight and explore some of the complexities inherent in the organizational buying process (see Figure 2.8).

It relies heavily on the process of stimulus and response, but it does bring out a number of important variables and depicts them in a systematic way. It also brings together a number of the known decision-making and behavioural theories and concepts which were current.

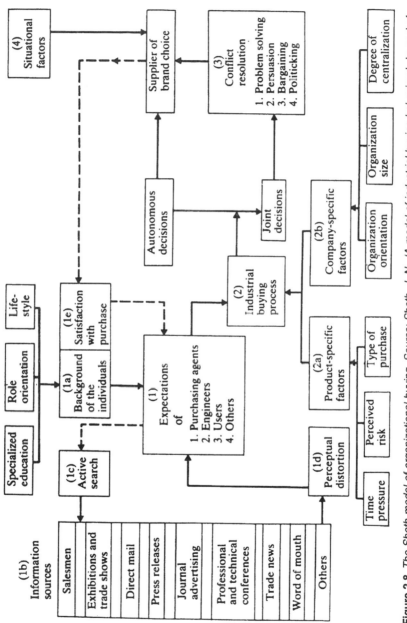

Figure 2.8 *The Sheth model of organizational buying. Source: Sheth, J. N., 'A model of industrial buying behaviour', Journal of Marketing, 37(4), October 1973*

The Webster and Wind model (Figure 2.9)

The Webster and Wind model[11] recognizes the importance of a number of potential players in the process. A number of other individuals and groups in a 'buying centre' may have influence or may have some decision-making powers which they will use in different ways according to the circumstances prevailing at the time.

Webster and Wind identified six roles within the buying centre. These were:

1 Users: those who initiate the buying process and may be the users or end customers.

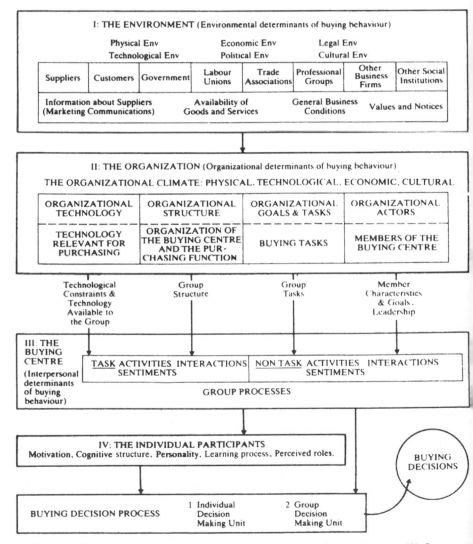

Figure 2.9 *Webster and Wind model of organizational buying behaviour. Source: W. O. Webster and Y. Wind,* Organizational Buying Behaviour, *Prentice-Hall, 1972*

2 Influencers: this group may include technical or other experts and other people not necessarily involved in the actual purchase whose views may be sought and carefully considered.

3 Deciders: individuals or groups who make the actual decision but may not be easy to identify as the decision may be made informally.

4 Approvers: where a formal authorization of the purchase is required and where the deciders give informal approval, the approvers will authorize the purchase decision.

5 Buyers: the individuals or departments who have the formal authority to buy and who negotiate the price and other details.

6 Gatekeepers: they play an interesting but often necessary role as the people who may stop you, the supplier, from reaching other members of the 'buying centre'.

Other models

Source loyalty model

This model by Webster and Wind suggests that there is a strong tendency for buyers to favour past suppliers. This is supported by the actions of many buyers but does not explain the process of locating and selecting the supplier in the first place.

Supply chain model

Suppliers are recognizing the value of the supply chain – suppliers of materials or parts to a manufacturer are taking part in the chain of supply which ends with the customer of the final manufacturer. In the Just-In-Time management system, suppliers and manufacturer work in partnership, and with very tight time scales and very high standards of quality. Response to customer needs becomes vital along with the whole chain.

Summary – How close are we to our customers, now?

There are many ways of describing our customers which can help us understand more about them and about how they purchase our products or services. We have reviewed a number of models which map out the processes which customers may go through before they reach a purchasing decision. In the consumer field as well as in organizations, there may be more than one person involved in the decision-making process. Our task as suppliers of products or services is to recognize these ingredients and to learn how we can use them to increase our customer base and improve the quality of what we supply, as well as increase levels of customer satisfaction.

Competence self-assessment

1   Describe the chain of people in your organization who represent your customers and suppliers when you carry out two of your main responsibilities.

2   Describe the chain of suppliers and customers in a manufacturing business such as cars.

3   Describe the chain of suppliers and customers in a service business such as air travel.

4   Prepare a profile of an individual customer who might buy one of your organization's products or services.

5   Prepare a profile of the head of a department who represents one of your most important internal customers.

6   What are the most important factors affecting you as a consumer if you are buying a car, a stereo system, a jar of coffee or a personal gift for your partner?

7   What are the most important factors affecting you as a business customer if you are buying office equipment, company cars or contract catering?

8   Using the example of the service to the accounts department on page 18, describe how you might improve your service to an internal department. How would this benefit your own department?

9   Identify the STEP factors affecting your organization's customers.

10   Using one of the purchasing process models in this chapter, describe the process for buying a package holiday and a contract distribution service.

11   Select three current television commercials for consumer products and describe the type of consumer at whom the commercial is aimed. Use the consumer buying factors described in this chapter.

12   Write a memo to a head of department with whom you deal regularly, outlining how you intend to improve your service to that department. List all the buying factors the head of department will take into account when assessing your proposal.

References

1 Ohmae, K. (1982) *The Mind of the Strategist*, Penguin, New York, p. 109.
2 Wells, W. D. and Gubar, G. (1966) Lifecycle concepts in marketing research, *Journal of Marketing Research*, November, p. 362.
3 Kotler, P. (1988), *The Principles of Marketing, Analysis, Planning, Implementation and Control* (6th edn), Prentice-Hall, New Jersey.
4 Mitchell, A. (1983) *The Nine American Life Styles*, Macmillan, New York.
5 Maslow, A. H. (1954) *Motivation and Personality*, Harper and Row, New York.
6 Howard J. A. and Sheth, J. N. (1969) *The Theory of Buyer Behaviour*, John Wiley, New York.
7 Engel, J., Kollat, D. and Blackwell, R. (1978) *Consumer Behaviour*, Dryden Press, New York.
8 Sheth, J. N. (1974) *Models of Buyer Behaviour*, Harper and Row, New York.
9 Kotler, Philip *op. cit.*
10 Sheth, J. N. (1973) A model of industrial buyer behaviour, *Journal of Marketing Research*, October.
11 Webster, W. and Wind, Y. (1972) *Organizational Buyer Behaviour*, Prentice-Hall, New Jersey.

3 From customers to markets

Why this chapter is important

Although we should aim to achieve the highest levels of customer satisfaction with all our customers, scarce resources mean that we are unlikely to achieve this. However, by dividing our customers into groups, we can identify which are the most important and which we can best satisfy with our existing resources. This chapter will help you focus on those priorities by providing you with guidelines on grouping customers into 'segments' and identifying important buying factors. You will be able to target improvement programmes on specific groups of customers to achieve the optimum business benefit. This will ensure that you do not waste valuable resources on customers or markets that do not offer good long-term potential. The chapter explains how research can be used to support your decisions on market segmentation and gives guidelines on the type of research that is appropriate to different customer segmentation tasks.

First, find your market

I have encountered a number of desperate sales people who have tried to sell me things that I have not wanted. What these people could not understand was that I was not in their target market. Why have these people been so persistent? Have they perhaps been taught how to overcome objections rather than to discover the real needs of their customers? They have been led to believe that virtually anybody and everybody is in their target market.

Previous chapters have emphasized the value of getting to know your customers. It is important to find a way of grouping customers together so that we can understand the different groups we serve and how we can reach others like them.

Grouping customers together provides a number of benefits:

■ We can deal with their needs more effectively.
■ We can find out more about each group.
■ We can find others who share their characteristics so that we can sell more.

The process of grouping people together is called 'segmentation': taking all of your customers and sub-dividing them into sub-sets called segments.

Why segment your markets?

Wind and Cardozo[1] provide a useful definition of segmentation:

> A group of present or potential customers with some common characteristic which is relevant in explaining (and predicting) their response to a supplier's marketing stimuli.

Market segments usually contain people with more than one shared characteristic and they have potential beyond their response to marketing stimuli. They are a descriptive instrument which helps you to understand and explain your markets, they are the means by which you can target services, products, messages and they are a valuable method of analysing markets. There are four main reasons for segmenting markets:

1 To help you gain a competitive edge.
2 To help you concentrate your marketing efforts on one or more specific groups with market potential.
3 To help you monitor competitive activity – why competitors are succeeding and why you are succeeding.
4 To help you improve business efficiency – if you analyse each customer's level of business, you will find that a large proportion of your sales are concentrated in the hands of a small number of customers. The phenomenon where something like 80 per cent of your sales are concentrated in the hands of 20 per cent of your total customers is often known as the Pareto principle.

Types of segmentation in consumer markets

By attributes

It is possible to use almost any attribute or combination of attributes to carry out segmentation, and any of the factors in the chapter on buyer behaviour could be used. These sub-divisions are mainly characteristics about purchasers which tell us something about them which is independent of the fact that they are your customers.

Here are some examples of segmentation in what appear to be mass markets:

- Football clubs opening family enclosures to attract a family audience during one of the worst periods of football hooliganism.
- Special editions of mass-market cars to appeal to drivers who want something different, but at mass-market prices.
- Environmentally friendly cosmetics aimed at caring consumers.
- Prestige instant coffees from specialist manufacturers appealing to people who prefer 'real' coffee.
- Regional beers from national brewing groups to win back beer enthusiasts.
- Cider, specially packaged to appeal to younger drinkers.

By buying behaviour

An alternative route is to use customers' buying behaviour. Categories can include:

■ Frequency of purchase.
■ Value of purchases.
■ Purchase only one brand.
■ Consistently switch brands.

The strategy for dealing with this type of segmentation includes not just the physical product or service, but its packaging, distribution and purchase. Some examples will illustrate this:

■ The introduction of shoppers' clubs by cash and carry wholesalers who traditionally dealt with trade only. The clubs recognize a consumer need to make savings through bulk purchase.
■ Petrol promotional schemes to build loyalty to a petrol brand or service station.
■ Interest-free credit schemes for major purchases such as electrical goods or cars.
■ Range extensions for customers who are loyal to one brand, speciality ice creams and desserts, for example, from a brand leader.

Types of segmentation in business markets

By type of organization

Organizations can be segmented in a number of ways:

■ Sector or industry.
■ Size.
■ Order value.
■ Centralized buying.
■ Strategic importance of business.
■ New customers.

A building services company, specializing in computer rooms and hi-tech buildings, surveyed its potential market to identify the major market segments and the key buying factors. Telephone researchers asked respondents to describe their purchasing procedures and to indicate the most important supplier attributes. Their research indicated a number of segments that were worth developing further:

■ Large national organizations with centralized buying wanted to deal with a single substantial national supplier who could provide their regional outlets with a local service.

- Organizations with decentralized buying wanted to deal with the local branch of a national organization rather than a small local company.
- Most of the respondents wanted to deal with a quality-led supplier (the company was BS 5750 registered).
- Buyers in the public sector looked for quality and value for money.

This information enabled the company to develop different strategies for different segments of the market so that they could reach a range of different customer needs.

Segmentation within organizations

It is also possible to segment your markets within individual organizations:

- Departments.
- Functions.
- Areas of responsibility.
- Direct or indirect contact with external customers.
- Financial and non-financial responsibilities.
- Internal or external customers.

A broadly based professional services company offering training or consultancy might use this approach to identify different business opportunities within the same organization:

- Strategic consultancy to the senior management team.
- Logistics consultancy to the distribution department.
- Product development consultancy to the marketing department.
- Human resources development to the personnel department
- Quality consultancy to the manufacturing department.
- IT consultancy to the IT department.

Although the consultancy is dealing with just one organization, there are many different customers within that organization, each with different needs.

Types of segmentation in internal markets

In internal markets the segments are usually defined in relation to your position and function. There are a number of useful ways in which you can segment customers to reflect your priorities:

- Customers who help you carry out your job.
- Customers who help you maintain good relations with your superiors.
- Customers who can make your life easier.
- Customers who are important to career development.

You can also segment internal customers by:

■ Location – by department, division or organization.
■ Their ability to affect the quality of service to external customers.

The computing services department of a local government organization provides services to a number of different customers, each with its own specific information requirements. These include:

■ Revenue collection systems for the housing department.
■ Senior management information systems.
■ Design and archive systems for the planning department.
■ Office administration systems for all departments.

Guidelines for segmentation

The number of criteria which could be used is almost endless and, to make sense of segmentation, there should be some rules or guidelines which we can all follow. The most important of these are:

■ Size.
■ Identity.
■ Relevance.
■ Access.

Size of segment

Is the segment large enough to warrant your marketing efforts?

The UK bearing industry, in common with many components manufacturers, found that they were being threatened by competition from the Japanese and Eastern Bloc countries. The new competitors attacked narrowly defined markets where volumes were high and price was a key issue. The UK manufacturers responded by automating the production of their high volume product ranges and also increasing their marketing effort in 'specials' – low volume, high quality bearings made to order. Although their competitors showed no real interest in the 'specials' segment, there was not sufficient potential in the segments to support a viable long-term business and the bearing companies had to adopt different strategies.

Identity

Can you clearly identify the constituents of the segment? Does it have predominant characteristics which distinguish it from other segments?

During the running boom of the 1980s, a number of magazines were launched to take advantage of a new market. *Athletics Weekly* was a long-established and respected magazine written for club athletes. However, the growth of fun runs, inspired by events like the London

Marathon, appealed to a new type of runner who was less serious and was unlikely to belong to one of the established clubs. *Running* magazine was launched to appeal to that market. It was designed and written as a consumer magazine and featured material and advertisements appealing to health-conscious lifestyle runners, rather than to the serious athlete. *Athletics Weekly* adopted a stronger consumer design, but retained its editorial policy of serious club athletics and both magazines continue to succeed because they appeal to clearly defined segments of the market.

Relevance

Segmentation must be relevant to the product or service you are marketing.

For example, the ownership of more than one TV may correspond closely with the ownership of computer games machines. However, this relationship alone is not enough either to identify the segment or to explain it.

Access

Can you communicate with the segment in a cost-effective way?

Desktop publishing has led to the growth of specialist publishing operations, serving tightly defined markets. In theory, there is a publication or other form of communication to reach any market segment, however small, but the cost of reaching those prospects cost effectively must be carefully calculated.

Targeting

The purpose of segmentation is to help you reach key groups of customers. The process of identifying and trying to reach them is called targeting. There are three strategies for targeting segments of your market:

1 Full coverage.
2 Multiple segments.
3 Single segment.

Full coverage

You aim for maximum coverage and ignore segments. This approach used to be called mass marketing and would be regarded by many marketers as no marketing at all. The approach assumes that you will market one product to everyone, promote to everyone using the same message, reaching everywhere, distributing through every type and size of retail outlet. With the inherent economies of scale in manufacture and the apparently low cost of advertising, there can be financial advantages in this approach.

Many commodity products use this strategy as a starting point to expand the whole market for their products. The work of organizations like the Dairy Council and the Meat Marketing Board in raising public awareness and increasing distribution provides a valuable basis for individual suppliers to pursue their segmentation policies, but there are few manufacturers with the weight to tackle that type of mass marketing on their own.

Multiple segments

You aim your efforts at more than one segment at a time, selling the same product but meeting the needs of each group through different product benefits. Private healthcare, for example, is marketed at a number of different levels. Individual or family policies are marketed directly to consumers. The same policies are sold to companies who provide healthcare as an employee benefit. The basic product is the same, but the corporate scheme offers companies an additional range of business benefits, such as improved employee relations, tax advantages and opportunities to attract new recruits.

Single segment

This can be the simplest strategy, assuming that the size of the segment is large enough to be profitable.

The Maldon Crystal Salt Company is a family business which has been handed down through several generations. The company produces and markets a very pure form of salt with a special flavour. The product has traditionally been marketed through health-food stores and aimed at a limited market. However, with the growth of interest in healthy eating, the product has gained distribution in a number of leading supermarkets, as well as speciality food stores. It remains a product aimed at a single segment, but it has grown by increasing distribution.

Choosing your targeting strategy

You should consider the following criteria before selecting your segmentation strategy:

- Does your market contain customers with few or no significant differences? Is it worth segmenting?
- Is it too early to segment or to use segmentation because your product, service or organization is too new?

- Does your product or service appear to be a commodity? The more like a commodity it is, the less useful segmentation will be.
- Can you see competitive advantage in segmenting?
- Do you have the staff and financial resources to help you fulfil your chosen strategy?

Gathering information

We now need to explore the role of information further and see how we can gather the information before we assess how we might improve our services to customers.

The process begins with research. Research gathers many different types of data which we can process into information. I make this distinction between data and information because the two terms are readily confused and in research it is important to distinguish between them. Research gathers data – basic unprocessed facts.

For example, we might gather data which tells us that 80 per cent of children in the UK like the taste of sugar or that 85 per cent of processed savoury snacks for children contain sugar or other sweeteners. If we put those two pieces of information together, we might conjecture that manufacturers of processed savoury products for the children's market in the UK put sweetener into their products to make them more attractive to their customers. This would be useful information to a company contemplating entry into the children's savoury snack market in the UK.

Research does more than gather information. It is there to help you make decisions, to solve problems and to monitor your progress or that of your competitors.

Research can be used to tackle problems in a number of areas:

- External markets or competitors.
- Products or services.
- Customers.
- Sales operations and distribution.
- Communications.

External markets or competitors

Research can provide you with data on:

- Economic, business, political trends and forecasts.
- Social and technological trends and developments.
- Competitors.
- Sales and consumption.

When car manufacturers are developing new models, they may be trying to predict market conditions four or five years ahead and they take external conditions into account. Key factors might include:

- The impact of environmental legislation on engine design.
- The globalization of world markets, where a single model such as the Ford Mondeo may be more appropriate than a range of models for different regions.
- Fuel supply conditions: the oil crises of recent years contributed, in part, to the drive for fuel-efficient engines and alternative power units.
- Consumer strength in areas such as safety and value for money.

Product or service research

New products and services

Research can help you to:

- Generate new ideas or concepts.
- Select and develop promising ideas.
- Identify markets or segments.
- Identify the key attributes which would make the new product or service appealing to selected markets.
- Develop product attributes, refine its design and finish.
- Test plans. While developing a marketing plan, research can help you test the plan and the marketing strategies.
- Name the new product or service.
- Set a price for it.
- Assist in planning its distribution.
- Predict sales.
- Design and target the advertising.
- Assess its success and refine it further before launching it nationally or cancel it.

An industrial paint manufacturer wanted to change market habits by charging customers for colour information which had traditionally been provided free. Before planning the launch, the company held a series of customer focus groups to gauge market reaction to the new service. The focus groups gave valuable information on:

- Customer attitudes to charges on a previously free service.
- The price the market would be prepared to pay.
- The benefits customers would be looking for.
- Customer attitudes to the quality of the colour service.

As a result of that research, the company was able to put together a package of services which appealed to the market and there was no adverse reaction to the charges.

Existing products and services

Everything outlined in the previous section could be carried out on existing products or services. However, research on existing products or services tends to concentrate more on the problems of continuing to manage them and less on development. In this area research helps you to:

- Monitor your products and services.
- Compare your products or services with existing ones and newly launched ones.
- Redesign or repackage what you sell.
- Test effects of these and other changes such as price.
- Monitor advertising and promotions.
- Develop and refine advertising messages.
- Select advertising media.
- Target the advertising messages to the selected segments.

A European construction equipment manufacturer researched the market for replacement parts and found that branding and customer service was becoming increasingly important as construction equipment grew more complex and the cost of breakdown grew higher. As a result of the research, the manufacturer redeveloped its network of service depots, operated a company-wide training programme and repackaged all of its products to put greater emphasis on the brand name. A direct mail and advertising campaign aimed at construction companies encouraged them to try the new service available through the depots.

Customer research

Research can help you identify:

- The size of your market.
- What sorts of people your market consists of.
- Market potential.
- Trends and market share.
- What your customers think of your organization and its products or services.

A company specializing in processing credit card transactions was originally owned by a group of banks, but subsequently became an independent company. Research into customer perceptions indicated that many potential customers believed the company was still an internal bank department and that limited their growth potential. By using the research, they were able to develop a communications strategy which repositioned them as a successful independent company and allowed them to expand their market.

Sales operation and distribution research

Research can help you:

- Monitor your salesforce's effectiveness.
- Ensure that territories are properly defined and covered.

- Gather and interpret sales statistics.
- Produce forecasts.
- Provide goal-oriented incentives.
- Develop sales training programmes to improve weaknesses in performance.

A regional electricity company operating a network of showrooms, researched levels of product knowledge and motivation among the showroom salesforce. The research indicated a number of problems which limited the opportunities for revenue growth and expansion. The company was able to put together a package of training and incentive programmes in conjunction with manufacturers whose products they were distributing. The manufacturers were willing to cooperate because the electricity company had presented them with a fully researched proposal, rather than a simple demand for support. Research can also help you manage your distribution network by allowing you to:

- Test new channels of distribution.
- Understand the attitudes of the trade.
- Understand the effects on the trade of changes in your distribution policy.
- Evaluate current distribution channels.

The government has announced on several occasions that it would like to change the way it distributes social security benefits. It has considered a number of alternatives including direct credits to customers' bank accounts and a move away from the Post Office. As well as researching customer attitudes to these changes, the government also has to take into account the views of the Post Office and the banks who would handle future transactions.

Communications research

Communications covers a wide range of activities including advertising and other forms of promotion, company image, sales, merchandising, packaging, and point-of-sale display. Research can help you identify:

- How customers perceive your product or service.
- What messages need to be communicated.
- How to reach your target audience.
- Through which media, when and where should you communicate.
- The effectiveness of your communications.

A manufacturing company decided to reposition itself as a services organization. It currently offered its customers maintenance services and a limited amount of consultancy. After restructuring its service department and developing a range of service products, it decided to carry out a communications audit to identify the key communications tasks. The audit was carried out by an independent consultancy and measured factors such as:

- Customer awareness of the importance of professional services.
- Customer awareness of the supplier's service capability.
- Salesforce awareness of the company's service capability.
- The level of service messages in current communications.

The audit helped the company to develop important messages and to set benchmarks which would identify the level of communications needed to influence the most important audiences.

Research data

There are two basic types of data: 'Primary' and 'Secondary'. Primary data is collected for a specific purpose, while secondary data is collected for more general purposes. Secondary data is easier to obtain but is presented in forms which are often less flexible than your own primary data. Collection and analysis of secondary data usually come under the heading of 'desk' research.

Secondary data

All data share one characteristic. The data's value is directly related to the quality of the source. Good desk research relies just as much on good quality data as it does on the quality of the analysis. You can obtain secondary data from 'Internal' or 'External' sources. Internal data sources can be found anywhere in your organization. The more your organization is aware of the value of its internal data, the more likely it is that it will operate some form of management information system and, if it is really enlightened, it will have a marketing information system.

Internal secondary data

Secondary data may not fit your exact requirements; for example, management information systems may have sales performance data by month or quarter, by product and region and perhaps by individual sales representative, but this data may not have the detail or take into account information which is of importance to a marketing department. The following example shows how data can be turned into useful information.

In the shipping industry, data from manifests generated by computerized container control systems can provide valuable market information. A ship's manifest contains the details of every item of cargo placed on the ship, its origins and its destination. Cargo details include type and description of the cargo, its size and weight and its value in terms of how much it cost to ship. This data can be used to create reports which cover:

- What was shipped to each destination on each cargo route.
- Details of the sales region where the cargo originated.
- The value of the cargo and its contribution to the total sales from each region.
- Shippers by value per average unit of cargo and by region.
- New shippers, lapsed customers and prospects.
- Competitive activity.

External secondary data

External secondary data is collected by other organizations, and may be gathered for purposes not relevant to your intended use. In the UK, we have a wide variety of sources to choose from, and Tull and Hawkins[2] suggested that these sources could be grouped into five main categories:

1 Computer databases.
2 Associations.
3 Government agencies.
4 Syndicated services.
5 Other sources.

Commercial databases

There is a wide range of databases containing company and market information which can be obtained on-line via a modem and telephone line. Examples include:

- Extel.
- BRAD (British Rate and Data).
- Kompass (UK).
- Times 1000.
- Datastream.
- Who Owns Whom.

Non-commercial databases

These include:

- University departments.
- Organizations such as the SSRC (Social Science Research Council).
- Library publication databases.
- University and college libraries.

Associations

Almost every association has some form of database or recording system to help them record, locate and communicate with their members. There are a number of reference books, indexes and digests which include lists and details of such associations, including:

■ Trade and commerce associations.
■ Employer and employee associations.
■ Trade unions.
■ Professional institutions.
■ Charities.
■ Voluntary organizations.

Government agencies

The government publication *The Guide to Official Statistics* (available from HMSO) is published every year and is a useful starting point for data on specific subjects. These agencies can be local, regional, national or international/foreign government sources. The range of data includes:

■ Census data.
■ Data from surveys including the national household expenditure survey, health and education surveys.
■ Employment data.
■ Price indices.
■ General economic data.
■ Import and export data.
■ Special studies on markets or industries.
■ Local and national plans.
■ European Community data and reports.

Syndicated services

The Market Research Society Handbook published by the Market Research Society includes details of a wide variety of commercial and non-commercial sources, including:

■ Published data.
■ Published analyses and reports.
■ Computerized databases available on-line and on disc.
■ Research summaries and indexes.

Other published sources

Libraries hold an enormous range of published materials and have a variety of data retrieval systems. You can also keep yourself informed through publications such as the *Economist*, the *Financial Times*, and radio and television current affairs and business programmes. In addition to this, you can obtain summaries of articles or whole publications on computer.

Specialist commercial and professional sources

There are three main sources:

1 Databases used by particular professions, for example, the legal profession and medical and scientific associations.
2 Professional databases containing details of mailing lists which link commercial data to a geo-demographic classification system, the electoral role and the national postal code file.
3 Company databases which are held and managed by database management companies.

Problems with secondary data

With data sources still increasing, there is a risk of drowning in excess data. Proper objectives, a clear set of standards for the data you want to use and a determination to avoid duplication will help avoid data overload. Here is a summary of the major considerations in selecting sources:

■ Understand why the data was collected in the first place.
■ Find out how it was collected, including the sampling and survey design, questionnaire design, methodology, and the approach to analysis.
■ Be certain that you trust the source's integrity.

Primary data

Every manager collects primary data. Chapter 4 focuses on the ways in which managers collect and evaluate data which directly affects their own job.

Competence self-assessment

1 List all the internal customers you deal with. How would you group them into segments? What factors would you use to segment your markets?

2 Rank your market segments in order of importance. What factors would you use to prioritize the segments?

3 The Inland Revenue has recently introduced a new-look assessment form, researched and designed by a leading communications consultancy for ease of use. What does this tell you about the Inland Revenue's attitude to its 'customers'? Which segments of their market would most benefit from the new form?

4 Look at your organization's product range. What are the most important segments for your products and what are the key characteristics of the segments.

5 Take a product or service that is important to your business. If you were the supplier, how would you classify your organization?

6 Can you identify any market segments currently served by your company which you feel have poor long-term potential? What factors lead you to believe this?

7 If you were responsible for launching a new product in your organization, what external factors would you research? Assume the product is an extension of your existing range.

8 You want to improve the service your department offers to internal customers. What research data is available to support your planning, and what other information do you need to find out?

9 Your department is under-funded, constantly criticized and threatened with closure. However, you feel that it performs a vital role and is misunderstood. Outline a research programme to identify with whom you should be communicating and what perception they hold of you.

10 What sort of secondary data is held by your organization and how can you access it?

References

1 Wind, Y., Yoram, J. and Cardozo, R. (1974) Industrial Marketing Segmentation, Industrial Marketing Management, **3**, p. 155.
2 Tull, D. S and Hawkins, D. I. (1987) *Marketing Research: Measurement and Method* (4th edn), Collier Macmillan, London.

4 Informal research

Why this chapter is important

There is no better form of research than looking at a problem or opportunity through your customer's eyes. This chapter explains how to take that point of view and how to help the customer provide you with all the information you need to assess their requirements. Listening and observing, however, is only the starting point. Unless you take action, your research will be wasted.

Closer to your customers

This chapter is separate from the traditional research chapters for two reasons. First, it is research you will do yourself and, second, it forms a bridge between the proactive and the responsive approaches to marketing that I am covering in this book. Tom Peters in his book *Thriving on Chaos*[1] says that there are four elements to the process of keeping close to your customers. These are:

1 Going to your customers.
2 Looking at them.
3 Listening to them.
4 Providing them with feedback.

I would add a fifth element – Action – and suggest that it comes between listening and feedback. I would also suggest that it really looks like Figure 4.1.

If you consider each part of the loop you can see clearly that this loop is not simply aimed at existing customers, it is for all customers and is relevant to us all.

Going to your customers

Knowing who your customers are does not mean that you actually know them! It does not mean that you have taken the time to meet any of them. How often have you heard the complaint that customers are a nuisance and that life would be better without them. So, the first step is to go to your customers, meet them and find out about them. Be interested in them, in their view of what they do and how you fit into their framework. Going to your customers will help you come back to your own department with a fresh vision.

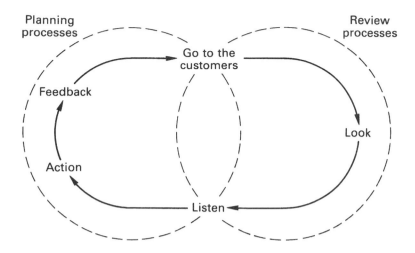

Figure 4.1 *The customer responsive marketing loop*

Opportunities to meet customers

Although we are recommending that you go to your customers, this is not always possible. While the salesforce are in regular, direct contact with customers, their motives and interests are different. As a manager in contact with a customer, your role is not to persuade, but to listen. To do that, you need opportunities to meet. Banks show us, through their television commercials, how their business managers roll up their sleeves and meet customers on site to get a first hand view of the business.

- If you can visit your customer's premises, that provides an ideal opportunity to see your product or service in action.
- You may arrange customer visits to your premises. That gives you their undivided attention to hear about their needs. Make sure that visitors have an opportunity to meet the staff and the managers who are working on their business.
- Technical liaison enables customers and suppliers to develop close working relationships and gain a better understanding of each other's needs.
- In partnership situations, where there is a high degree of cooperation between customer and supplier, project teams, consisting of people from different disciplines in both organizations, work together to tackle specific problems and opportunities.
- Membership of user groups or industry liaison groups provides an opportunity for formal and informal contact with customers.
- Introduce a programme of customer care visits. This is the most positive move you can make. Tell your customers that you want to find out about their business and discuss any concerns they might have.

It may be just as hard to build up a level of customer contact within an organization. Rigid departmental structures or inflexible procedures may keep people working in isolated compartments.

A European automotive components manufacturer recognized the risks in maintaining separate teams, and took the opportunity to build a level of cooperation that crossed national boundaries. Whenever they opened a new plant, they got together multi-disciplinary teams from all their plants to support the new plant. The teams discussed best practice and shared their own successes and failures. They worked with the new plant's management team during the planning and commissioning stages to ensure that the new plant reflected the collective experience of the whole group. The result was an organization that could bring a new plant on stream rapidly and provide the plant's customers with a quality service from day one.

A way of looking

By meeting your customers at first hand, you will see what your customers are really looking for from you and look with your customers' eyes at what you provide.

A consultant, working with a local health authority to improve current services and develop new ones to fit in with the Patients' Charter, was asked to help train staff in the reception and outpatient departments to deal with aggressive and disruptive customers. The consultant asked why the customers tended to be aggressive and was told that it was to be expected. Before agreeing to train the staff the consultant asked the director to show him around the reception area. The director explained the reception procedures, and pointed out that the receptionists had the problem not the customers, they were the ones who caused the problems.

The consultant then talked the director through the process that some patients might face if they had an accident – travelling on two buses to the hospital, finding their way through the maze to this department, then waiting half an hour to explain to the receptionist what was wrong and up to two hours to be seen, with the knowledge that they are going to have to repeat the journey in reverse to get home. He then asked the director what features the reception department had which helped make the customers' wait a more pleasant one. The director had always known the substance of what had been said but had never considered it and had never seen it as relevant. The consultant took on the training project, but he also helped change the process by which customers were dealt with, and he helped to change the environment of the waiting room completely.

He had already carried out his own version of looking at customers and looking with them. He began, not at the final delivery of the service, the treatment, but at the beginning of the customers' experience of going to the hospital and being served.

When you look at your customers you should try to find the beginning of their experience of your products or services. Write a list to consider the positive and negative aspects which might be encountered by your customers at each stage. You will see that your service to others has elements which are under your direct control and other elements where you depend on others for the quality of the services. Any improvement of your service is likely to involve direct action on your part and a management of your relationship with those on whose services you depend.

Listening

Tom Peters[2] christened the form of listening which we should adopt 'naive listening'. It requires that you adopt a frame of mind which allows you to hear what the other person is saying. Don't give a speedy answer to any question or problem. Make certain that you are hearing what is being said. If someone tells you they wish you could deliver on Wednesdays rather than Thursdays, don't answer by explaining why it has to be Thursday. Consider what is being said. What is that person's underlying reason for preferring Wednesday and is it a temporary or permanent requirement? You may be able to help your customer on a temporary basis or find some other solution to the customer's underlying problem.

You must leave your customers with a conviction that you hear what they say. Even if you can do nothing about their problem, they will know that you understand and are willing to help. Without this attitude you will not hear your customers and, conversely, your customers will not bother trying to tell you. It is a particularly British phenomenon that people who are dissatisfied with a product or service may never tell the supplier that they were unhappy. How many times have you been unhappy with an aspect of service in a restaurant or hotel and yet you have told no one who might have been able to change things? What you do instead is vow never to go there again. If someone had adopted a good listening attitude and was giving you the feeling that what you said was being heard, you might have told that person and something might have been done.

Asking questions

An important part of the listening process is asking questions. A good librarian knows that his or her customers know what they want but most of them do not know how to tell the librarian exactly what they want. So the librarian needs to know how to ask the questions to help find out the needs of each customer. Part of the skill of asking questions is in the listening, and part is in stopping yourself from asking 'What do I want to find out?' and rather ask 'What are you trying to tell me?' The first approach suggests that you already know and that you are trying to find evidence of this in what your customer says. The second assumes that you have to hear what is being said and work with the customer to help him or her to express their concerns or needs more clearly. By doing this, you are more likely to find out what your customer's priorities are and what is important to them about your product or service.

- Don't use questions which invite a simple yes or no answer, or questions which limit the customer's choice of answers.
- Start with open questions beginning with words like 'why' and 'how' and give the customer enough room to get his or her feelings and concerns or interests out into the open.
- Listen carefully and wait for them to finish, be sure that they have finished and check that what you have understood is what they believe they have said.
- If they have not already given their view of how things could be improved, seek their views now.
- If they have expressed their ideas of how to resolve or improve things ask them if they have any other ideas and always be listening and watching them.
- If they have no solutions or suggestions and you have some, or if you have a solution which you would prefer, you may well decide to ask them what their views on it are.

Now that you have gone to your customers and looked at them and with them, you will need to do something to improve things or respond to customer needs. You will also have to let them know what you are intending to do. You should also take the opportunity to share your findings with other people in the organization.

Reporting customer contact

The number of people who have an opportunity to make direct contact with customers is likely to be only a small proportion of the management team, let alone the entire workforce. Yet true customer satisfaction depends on the involvement of everyone in an organization, so customer contact and customer understanding must be shared.

There are a number of ways of achieving this:

- Circulating customer contact reports, visit reports, reviews, progress reports and other records to people with customer-facing responsibilities.
- Briefing other members of the management team on the meeting.

- Setting up project teams to respond to the customer contact.
- Setting up broadly based support teams to work with customer-facing staff.

Action

The first thing you will need to do is review what you have learned so far. This action is necessary to make certain that you have learned something useful and that any action you take will have been taken after due consideration. There may be things you can do straight away without causing disruption elsewhere and there will be actions which need consent or cooperation from others. Finally, you will need to use what you have learned within the context of your own or your department's plans. List out the problems and any solutions you might have and review them from the customer's point of view. To you there might be a major change which you see as being vital if you are to serve your customer appreciably better for years to come. However, this change may take time, and some other actions which require less time or resources may have a significant and immediate effect from the customer's point of view. What does the list look like from the customer's view point? How can you improve things from their point of view?

In summary, you need to learn to intervene where it matters from the customer's point of view and include the issues and needs into your planning process.

Feedback

If you respond to a customer's needs and requests and fail to point that out to him or her, it may go unnoticed and when the change is noticed it may be greeted with less enthusiasm than you would expect. However, if you tell the customer of the intended change and thank them for their help, and if you point out other changes which they can expect which were the direct result of their input, then the customer's attitude towards even the smallest changes will be significant. You will have shown your customer that you really do listen and that you care enough to do something about it as well! The chances are that you have earned commitment from that customer.

Feedback does not just happen once. Feedback should be part of a dialogue which you have initiated between yourself and your customers. You should continue to keep them informed and make certain that the channels of communication remain open for them to feed their views and feelings back to you. Feedback should also be part of your review procedure and should be included into your future plans.

Competence self-assessment

1   If you are not directly involved in sales, what opportunities do you have to meet customers?

2   How many other people in your organization – technical staff, senior executives, consultants – have opportunities to meet customers and do they take full advantage of the opportunities?

3   Does your organization have a set procedure for customer visits to your site? Who is included on the 'tour' and what could be done to improve contact and understanding between customers and the departments whose actions directly affect customer satisfaction?

4   Do staff who visit customers prepare visit reports, and if so, who receives copies? How do you think you could improve the reporting process?

5   You are preparing a proposal for improving your department's service to an internal customer. You have arranged to meet the head of the department for an informal meeting. Make a list of the questions you would like to ask at that meeting.

6   After the meeting, it is important to maintain contact with that head of department. Write a brief summary of the key points of your meeting. Outline a programme for maintaining effective contact through memos, progress reports and review meetings.

References

1 Peters, T. (1987) *Thriving on Chaos: Handbook for a Management Revolution*, Pan, London.
2 Peters, T. and Austin, N. (1986) *A Passion for Excellence, The Leadership Difference*, William Collins, Glasgow.

5 What are your customers getting?

Why this chapter is important

Part of the process of meeting customer needs is providing the right product or service. To do that, we need to understand the benefits our product or service offers the customers – what are they really buying from us? We also need to understand how our products are perceived in the market so that we can develop or change them to meet the changing needs of the market. By monitoring the way the market buys products like ours, we can develop strategies for planning our future product offerings. If we don't adapt, our business may not survive. This chapter describes a number of analytical tools and strategies for managing products and services for both internal and external markets.

Products, services – what are they?

According to Philip Kotler[1]:

A product is anything that can be offered to a market for attention, acquisition, use or consumption that might satisfy a want or need. It includes physical objects, services, persons, places, organizations and ideas.

Kotler says that products or services satisfy a want or a need. Car manufacturers claim that they do not sell cars, they sell the skills of their workforce, self-esteem, comfort, speed, safety, and style. The car is part of the medium through which these needs and wants are satisfied. You need the customer to help you answer the question 'what do you provide?' – even if you are holding the product in your hand!

Putting the product under the microscope

The model in Figure 5.1 suggests that products or services consist of the CORE product or service, the TANGIBLE product or service and the AUGMENTED product or service.

The CORE product or service

The core product of the Royal Mail is not stamps or courier services or even the postal system. It is the means of solving communications

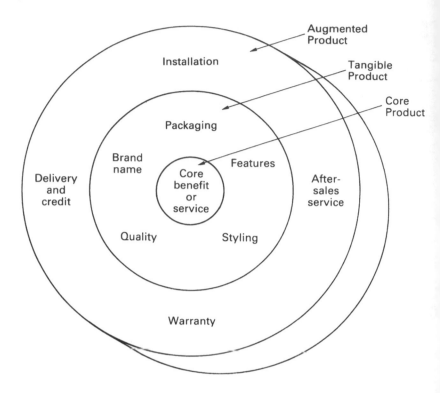

Figure 5.1 *Three levels of analysis of the product or service*

problems cheaply and effectively. Do toothpaste manufacturers simply sell toothpaste? They sell protection from tooth decay and they sell clean, fresh mouths. They identify the needs, fears and hopes of their customers and their products are designed to overcome their customers' concerns.

What is the core product or service of your department or your organization?

The TANGIBLE product or service

List every characteristic of what you provide. Your tangible product is the thing which satisfies your customer's needs or wants. So if you were manufacturing toothpaste you can list the following:

The product's composition.
Its design.
The quality of its ingredients.
Dispenser design.
Packaging design.
Research and development skills.

General staff expertise.
Staff attitude and commitment.
Its brand name and reputation.
The brand logo and identity.
The instructions.
The manufacturer's reputation.

You can also list specific details about a brand:

Available in a variety of sizes.
Sold in three different styles of dispenser.
Available in three different flavours.
Its ingredients are hypo-allergenic.
Quality controls are better than any other manufacturer.
The brand is available in all leading stores, supermarkets and chemists, as well as in the majority of minor retail outlets.
The tubes and other dispensers are environmentally friendly.
The product is not tested on animals.

The AUGMENTED product or service

What do you offer which adds value to the product – a guarantee or a free advice service, an extended warranty or a discount on the next consultation? In the example of the toothpaste, the augmented product might include the following:

The company has a dental helpline for all of its customers.
It has a money-back guarantee system if the customer is not satisfied with the product.
It works with individual dentists and dental organizations on dental care education.
It has a set of school dental-education packs for different age groups.
It carries out research on teeth, dental decay and techniques.
It funds several scholarships and awards.

What makes your products or services different?

In marketing, you will often hear references to a product or service's USP – the Unique Selling Proposition which makes your product or service stand out from those of your competitors. If there is little difference between your products and those of your competitors, you may find it difficult to compete. The simplest way of finding or confirming what your USPs are is to list those elements you have discovered when you were trying to identify your core, actual and augmented products or services, and compare them against your competitors. Can you identify those features which are both unique and attractive to your customers? Are they features which motivate your customers to buy?

Let your customer know

Look at what you listed as your tangible and augmented products or services and think about the benefits they hold for your customers. What needs do they satisfy? For example, British Telecom do not tell you that telephone messages are transmitted at a specific speed down the line, that they may be automatically routed through several exchanges and be subjected to a specific rate of error checks in a given space of time. You expect your call to encounter no problems, to have no interference and to be subject to no crossed lines or other hindrances. You are not interested in the technical details.

When you look for benefits in your lists of features, consider them from the customer's point of view. As an anonymous commentator put it:

Do not offer me things.
Do not offer me clothes. Offer me attractive looks.
Do not offer me shoes. Offer me comfort for my feet and the pleasure of walking.
Do not offer me books. Offer me hours of pleasure and the benefit of knowledge.
Do not offer me records. Offer me leisure and the sound of music.
Do not offer me furniture. Offer me comfort and the quietness of a cosy place.
Do not offer me things. Offer me ideas, emotions, feelings and benefits.
Please do not offer me things.

You don't have to write advertising slogans for your products or services. It is enough simply to translate the features into benefits.

Think about your organization, your department and even yourself as an integral part of the product or service. Examine your department and your organization from the point of view of your customers. Ask yourself how these personal aspects relate to your customers' needs, then try to find the features which serve these needs and define them. Finally, redefine them as benefits which will be easily understood by your customers.

Where is your product or service going?

Where do your products and services currently stand within the market?
Where are they going?
How can you manage them alongside your other products or services?
How can you develop new products or services?

Where are you now?

You must understand your position relative to that of your competitors to understand where you are and to direct your strategy to improve your position.

Positioning   Professor Yoram Wind[2] has identified six alternative bases for conducting a product or service positioning strategy. These are:

1 Positioning on specific product or service features. For example, brand x is regarded as being the best at removing stains.
2 Positioning on benefits, problems or needs. Brand x is thought of as the most environmentally friendly product. This meets a growing need in the marketplace.
3 Positioning for specific usage. Brand x is a necessity for heavy users: people hosting parties or large families, for example.
4 Positioning for user category. The product could be targeted specifically at members of environmental groups.
5 Positioning against another product. Brand x compares with the best-selling competitor and is cheaper.
6 Product class dissociation. Johnson & Johnson marketed their baby lotion primarily for babies, but identified a significant market among women who used it as a cleanser.

Mapping   There are simpler ways of looking at your position in the marketplace – mapping each product or service's position on a chart. Take two characteristics of the market which you know are important. Use your research to provide you with data on your competitors as well as your own product or service and plot them on a graph which has the two characteristics as the x and y axes. Calculate the overall average of the combined products or services and mark them as two lines on the graph (see Figure 5.2). This gives us four quadrants which we can use as a quick reference to help us read the graph or positioning map.

Figure 5.2 shows a real example taken from relatively old readership data. The vertical axis is the percentage of each paper's readership which can be classified as social grades A, B or C1. The average percentage of their total combined readership falling into any one of these class groups comes to just over 40 per cent. The horizontal axis is assigned to the percentage of each paper's readership which falls into the fifteen to thirty-four years-old age range. Less than 40 per cent of the total combined readership of the newspapers falls into that age range. By plotting each paper's position according to its percentage of readers in the class groups and the age range, you can begin to build up a picture of the differences between papers and you can also identify groups or clusters of papers who appear to be competing for broadly similar markets.

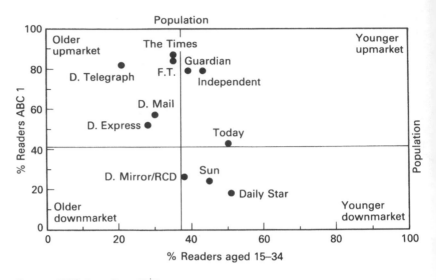

Source: NRS Jan.–Dec. 1989

Figure 5.2 *National daily newspapers – readership by social grade and age*

This approach helps you to segment your market; now go back to your lists of your product or service's features and benefits. If you have research which records respondents' feelings towards your own and your competitors' products or services it will probably be recorded as a score from one to five with one being 'Strongly agree' and five being 'Strongly disagree'. Select two statements which you think make your product or service important and use them as the vertical and horizontal axes. Place each product or service in its position on the graph and draw lines for the mean score of all respondents and examine your position on the map – how do you fare against your competitors?

You can also map basic performance and other business statistics in the same way and get some feel for your position in the marketplace. For example, you might be able to obtain profit, volume and revenue figures for the major players in your market. These and other basic data can be used to help you understand your competitive position.

Where to now?

The Ansoff Matrix

The Ansoff Matrix[3] shown in Figure 5.3 serves as a good basic tool for demonstrating where an organization may go and assessing the risk. It identifies four potential strategies:

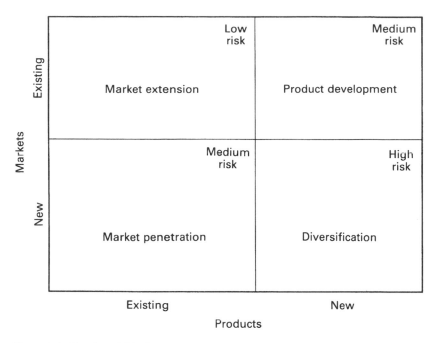

Figure 5.3 *The Ansoff Matrix*

1 Market penetration.
2 Market extension.
3 Diversification.
4 Product development.

Market penetration Getting more out of your current position. You market more of your product or service within your existing market – selling more to existing customers and selling to competitors' customers.

Market extension Finding new segments to sell to. These can be people in new regions or customers who buy your product or service for new reasons. For example, when Johnson & Johnson discovered the alternative use of their baby lotion, they carried out a market extension exercise.

Diversification The most extreme form of strategy where you have to employ both product or service development and market extension into new, possibly unknown, markets. There can be a high risk of failure because of poor understanding of the market, inappropriate products or high cost of market entry. Persil managed to diversify from detergents to washing-up liquids by product improvement, heavy advertising, good distribution and the proper use of their existing brand image. They succeeded in a market which was dominated by a well-established brand.

Product development   A less risk-laden strategy is to launch new or modified products in existing markets. The environmental concerns of the buying public opened up new possibilities for washing powder manufacturers in the late 1980s and early 1990s.

Risk

If you plan to make changes to your products or services you will have to consider the level of risk. Market penetration, market extension and product development share a common characteristic. They all keep one of the variables constant. They either keep the product constant or keep the market constant. The diversification option breaks what Ansoff calls the common 'thread' of the business and results in the organization venturing into unknown territory. This is why it is seen as the highest risk option. Ansoff outlined the factors which he believed were at the heart of the common threads:

■ The product–market scope. Stick to what you know best; many companies that have tried to diversify without considering the directions they were going with their diversification have become over-stretched.
■ The growth vector. Where are you heading with your products or services? This assumes that there is a logical direction which is determined by the products and services and is also dictated by the market.
■ The competitive advantage. You can see an aspect of your market or sector which you can use to strengthen your position and give you some competitive edge.

These threads point to ways of minimizing risk within the strategies described in Ansoff's matrix. Of course, when we analyse our position in our current market, we may find that the option with the highest risk is the one where we do not change! Our products or services may be out of date or suddenly challenged by a new alternative, or our customers may be demanding products or services which take into account their new concerns or needs.

Before you select your strategy ask:

■ What do your customers really demand?
■ What is your organization capable of doing to respond?
■ Consider your competitors.
■ Consider the rest of the external environment.

If we go back to the Persil example, you can see that the existing products were changed and developed to compete within the existing market. The introduction of a new product into a new market was diversification but there were common threads which strengthened the move:

- The new market had similar characteristics, so their product–market scope helped.
- They saw competitive advantages in moving into a new market with a new product.

Product life cycle

The life of your product or service changes as markets change, and customers' needs change over time, or new alternatives come onto the market. You will have to plan ahead to deal with these changes. The Product Life Cycle suggests that any given product or service is likely to proceed through a number of stages in its life, from birth to death, and it also suggests that the way in which we manage our products or services will determine whether we can extend and prolong its life. The Product Life Cycle in its basic form has five stages or phases which can be seen in Figure 5.4:

1 Introduction.
2 Growth.
3 Maturity.
4 Saturation.
5 Decline.

1 **Introduction** Growth can be slow and uncertain as customers test the product or service and approach it with the caution reserved for the new and unknown. Sales grow slowly and gradually.
2 **Growth** Sales begin to pick up rapidly as the customers become more familiar with the product or service and begin to recognize its benefits. This stage is also characteristically the point when competitors enter the market and stimulate interest and knowledge of the product or service.

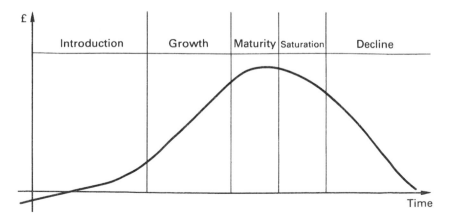

Figure 5.4 *The Product Life Cycle*

3 **Maturity** Almost every customer who needs it has it, few new customers are found and there is a certain amount of replacement activity within the market where, for example, old products are being discarded and new ones being bought.
4 **Saturation** The market is no longer enjoying growth and cannot support all of the suppliers who are competing for market share. This is when some suppliers go out of business and when price wars and other destructive actions make market conditions difficult for all suppliers.
5 **Decline** Here you will see sales drop off, suppliers drop out of the market and new products or services begin to appear as alternatives.

In real life, this pattern is far more complex. With a fashionable product the life cycle may take a year or two to work through from introduction to decline. These fashionable products tend also to be well distributed earlier than many other types of product and their growth is extremely rapid. However, when the market reaches maturity there tends to be few second purchases and the market limits are prone to be very clearly and tightly defined. Thus, saturation and decline are very rapid. Maturity can be delayed by changes or improvements, broadening the product's appeal or encouraging increased loyalty. This extended maturity can be seen in Figure 5.5.

The concept of the Product Life Cycles can be applied to the internal market, for example, in accountancy systems, computers, databases, personnel systems and even quality management systems. The introduction phase requires large amounts of effort and expenditure of resources and/or commitment, the growth phase occurs when it begins really to show its worth and provide business benefit. The maturity and saturation stages occur when it is an integrated part of the routine with the least amount of investment in time and effort and

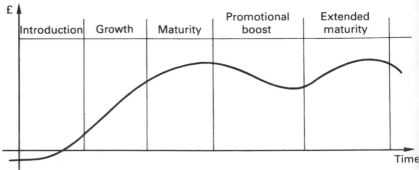

Figure 5.5 *Extensions of the Product Life Cycle*

the maximum return. At these stages alternatives will be tried out and replacement systems introduced. The decline stage is when a new product or service takes over.

Combinations or portfolios

In both internal and external markets, you will find that different products or services will be at different stages in their Product Life Cycle. Dealing with a combination of different products is sometimes called managing a portfolio of products. One of the most widely used concepts for managing product or service portfolios is the Boston Matrix (Figure 5.6). This was not developed to manage a portfolio of products or services, but was intended to help senior managers in large corporations to control and manage a number of disparate companies owned by the corporation. It was a tool for corporate strategy and management of semi-autonomous or independent profit centres.

The model consists of a matrix with two axes. The vertical axis represents the market growth rate. The model assumes that businesses in high growth-rate industries represent the most attractive investment because of their future growth and profit potential. In the original matrix, the mid-point dividing low from high growth rates was put at 10 per cent. However, in the UK, in many industries you would not expect such a high rate of growth. The horizontal axis represents the relative market share of each company or product. This is an indication

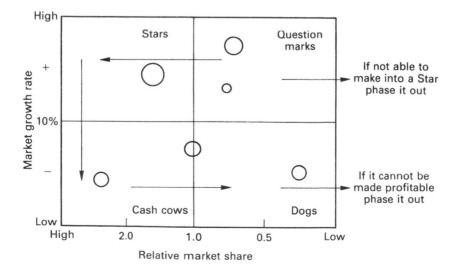

Figure 5.6 *The 'Boston Box' with desired movement of products through the matrix*

of the company or product's relative strength in the market and is computed by dividing the company or product's absolute share of the market by that of the leading company's share of the market. This share can be in value (£s) or in units. A score of 0.5 therefore means that the company or product's share is half that of the leading company while a score of 2.0 would mean that it was twice that of its nearest rival in the market.

A third dimension is introduced by giving each company or product a circle whose size relates to the actual volume of sales. When this matrix is used to manage portfolios of businesses, each business is called a Strategic Business Unit (SBU).

The matrix is sub-divided into four quadrants at points which are half-way between 'low' and 'high' on each axis:

1 Question marks.
2 Stars.
3 Cash cows.
4 Dogs.

Question marks   products, services or SBUs in high-growth markets with low market share. Do you invest to increase market share or do you pull out?

Stars   high market share in a high-growth market. You will still have to invest heavily to maintain position. This investment is likely to be returned as the product, service or SBU moves into the next quadrant.

Cash cows   market growth rate is now low, investment is also low and your product, service or SBU now becomes a cash generator. Because you are a leader in the market, you are enjoying the benefits of economies of scale and you do not have to invest heavily in expansion. High profit margins are enjoyed by cash cows.

Dogs   Cash cows which have lost their market share and have been overtaken or squeezed out by new products, services or companies. This is where you have low market share and you are in a low-growth market. You will need to decide whether you are going to reinvest in your dogs or phase them out.

This matrix is like a snapshot of your products, if you want to use it as a meaningful management tool you need to consider how you portfolio has changed over time and monitor progress as you intervene with appropriate strategies.

Developing products or services

New product development is a creative as well as a high-risk enterprise which involves many different skills. We are all, in our own way, product and service developers: we all have to develop, refine and even redefine what we provide to our customers. When you consider new product development, you should also consider development of existing products and services by:

- Enhancing what you already provide.
- Adding additional options.
- Extending the range.
- Redefining what you provide to existing customers or to prospects who might not have previously considered your products or services.

Listen to your customers. They tend to be the best people to find out about a product or service's imperfections and can also tell you what they might want. Listening to our customers may help stimulate ideas and suggest directions you should take in your investigations of new products or services. You may already have what they want but never have realized that customers in that sector or segment wanted it too. Alternatively, you may discover that what they want is available from another source. New product development can take the form of repositioning or acquisition.

Acquisition If you are considering buying-in the new product or service there are a number of different routes:

- Buying a company which produces the product you want or provides the services you need.
- Buying the patents or licence to manufacture or sell the products.

New product development If you are developing the new product yourself you may be working with others:

- Internal research and development department.
- Internal task force.
- Product development specialists.

Generating ideas

You can use a number of sources and techniques to generate new product ideas:

- Quality circles.
- Suggestions box.
- Electronic mail conferencing system.
- Your suppliers.
- Professional new product development agency.
- Competitors.
- Conferences, exhibitions and the media.

If you intend to develop ideas with the help of colleagues, there are a number of techniques to help, including brainstorming and attribute listing.

Brainstorming A group of people are put together in a room and given a problem or task to solve. As a group, they are expected to generate a given number of ideas within a certain time. There are no limits on what the members can suggest and no judgement is made on them. The person who runs the session is a facilitator who points the group in a direction and discourages particular views or ideas. All the ideas are recorded for evaluation and use later.

Attribute listing Attributes can be investigated and explored within the organization and with customers. Look at each element of a product or service and list its features before examining how it could be improved or changed.

To evaluate these new ideas, start off with a set of primary concerns and a set of lesser concerns which can be used as part of a gradual screening process. You now have ideas which fit your criteria. You will be working with designers, production engineers and others who can transform the theory into a product. At this stage you cannot relinquish your responsibilities to the technicians completely. They need your support and assistance to make certain that ideas are properly translated into specifications, products and production processes. At each stage, compromises can take place and priorities change because those working on the product are not aware or have not been regularly reminded of the real priorities by you or your colleagues.

The product programme then progresses through a number of stages:

- Where are you going to test-market the new product?
- How are you going to test it and what do you want to find out?
- Short run manufacturing.
- Test the complete marketing plan.
- Carry out essential refinements.
- Launch the product.

Competence self-assessment

1 'Car makers don't sell cars . . . they sell comfort, safety, speed and style.' What do you think your products are really offering your customers?

2 What is the USP of your organization's main product or service? How do your competitors' products differ from yours? What are their USPs?

3 Using the approach of 'Do not offer me things . . .' on page 60, what does your department offer your internal customers?

4 Six strategies for positioning a product are described on page 61. Take three consumer products you have bought recently and explain how they are positioned in each of the categories.

5 The section on mapping on page 61 suggests a number of exercises you can carry out. Complete these exercises.

6 Ansoff identifies four strategies for growth. How would you apply those strategies to help develop the scope of your department? What are the risks involved in each of the strategies?

7 What stage of the Product Life Cycle has the personal computer market reached? How do you think the market is likely to develop?

8 Can you apply the Product Life Cycle to the work of your department? Where do you think you are in the life cycle?

9 The Boston Matrix classifies products or companies as Question Marks, Stars, Cash Cows and Dogs. How would you classify your company's product range? If you are part of a large group, how would you classify the companies within the group?

10 What contribution could your department make to a new-product development programme? What perspective would you bring?

11 The Rover Group's origins lie in the separate companies that made up the British motor industry. Can you name some of the early constituent companies and groupings? Do you think that the acquisition strategy has worked consistently well?

12 Take one product or service in your organization that you would really like to improve. Who would you select for a brainstorming session and how would you guide the session?

References

1 Kotler, P. *op.cit.*
2 Wind, Y. J. (1982) *Product Policy: Concepts, Methods and Strategy*, Addison-Wesley, Reading, Mass., pp. 79–81.
3 Ansoff, I. (1965) *Corporate Strategy*, McGraw-Hill, New York.
4 Henderson, B. (1973) The experience curve reviewed: IV the growth share matrix or the product portfolio, *Boston Consulting Group Perspectives*, **135**, Boston, Mass.

6 The price, the cost and the value

Why this chapter is important

Even if you have a complete understanding of your customer and you have developed a product that meets every need, you may fail because the price is wrong. As a manager, you need to understand how the costs of various processes within the organization affect the final price the customer pays. You also need to understand how people value the product or service you provide. If you are in a competitive market where price is essential to winning business, how can you help add value so that your product or service represents better value for money? Increasingly, in both the public and private sectors, organizations are reviewing the real costs of providing services from within the organization and are asking external organizations to tender for the business. Are you certain that your department is providing real value for money? This chapter explains the basis of cost and price and outlines a number of strategies for dealing with different competitive situations.

Value and price

I have mentioned a number of factors which affect buying behaviour and I have pointed out some of the ways in which value is transferred. What you need to consider now is how price and value influence the buyer-behaviour system. To most people, price is a fairly obvious item. It can be used to help you decide between comparable products or services. When you make the comparison, however, you will also add your aspirations, desires, self-image, peer influences and so on as part of a hidden equation.

As a customer you will be trying to balance these factors in order to get either the best that you can afford or the closest to what you want. After the purchase has been made, you will begin to re-evaluate your purchase in the light of your experience of what you bought. If it fails to satisfy you or does not meet your expectations you will feel unhappy, displeased and perhaps even cheated. It will not have met your expectations in terms of its value or worth.

The same is also true for internal markets or situations where no monetary exchange takes place. The price which your customers pay for your services within your organization may include the time and effort the customer expends on briefing you or seeking your advice or help. The exchange between the two sides may be complicated and even obscure, but the value of what you provide will still be judged to some extent by the price paid and the quality of the provision. The benefits you provide and the needs you satisfy are directly related to the cost and how it compares with the customer's perception of its value.

Counting the cost

If you are calculating or setting a price you will have to go through three basic stages to reach the price you want:

1 Work out your costs with the help of your accountant or finance director.
2 Obtain market information so that you can understand the state of the market and what your competitors are doing.
3 Identify what customers or prospective customers think is value for money and what they feel is an acceptable price for your product or service.

Costs and your product or service

There are two types of cost: fixed and variable.

Fixed costs or overheads do not vary with the level of sales or production, they include:

■ Rent and business rates.
■ Salaries.
■ Heating and lighting.
■ Telephone rental.
■ Maintenance.
■ Office equipment.

Variable costs, which vary in proportion to production levels, include:

■ Raw materials.
■ Energy and labour.
■ Packaging and distribution.
■ Agency or sales commission.

The costs involved in producing a product or providing a service will have a direct effect on the price at which you sell the products or services, but they are outside the scope of this book.

Pricing and the customer

Traditional accounting methods allow only a passing reference to the customer and the market. You will need to consider the expectations of your existing or potential customers. If you set your price outside of the expected price range for your product or service, you could create uncertainty. I have talked about value for money and suggested that this includes image, expectations, actual prices and the quality of the product or service. If the price falls outside the expected range you must be able to justify this in the mind of the purchaser.

A company in the UK developed a new specialist alarm system which had many excellent features and offered state of the art home security. However, as the system was based on adaptations of services and equipment they were already selling, the initial investment costs were low so they decided to pitch the product at an affordable price. Sales started off very well but soon settled into a pattern of steady but slow growth – much slower than they had expected. They increased advertising and carried out very careful studies to ensure that they were reaching their target markets. After some time and much frustration, they carried out research to find out why people seemed to be buying more expensive packages with fewer features and poorer quality.

The research proved conclusively that the customers could not believe that such a system could be bought at the price for which it was being offered. They suspected 'hidden extras' or feared that the system must be of a poor quality, and so on. In other words, the customers felt that the price was outside the expected price confidence levels and they had built up a resistance to the product.

The company listened to the research very carefully, carried out some further research and relaunched their system onto the market at virtually double its original price. It is now a major force in that market sector.

Demand and price

The demand curve is intended to depict the relationship between price and quantity. It helps you ask the question 'How does price affect the quantity sold?' by creating a graph with price as the vertical axis and quantity sold as the horizontal axis (see Figure 6.1).

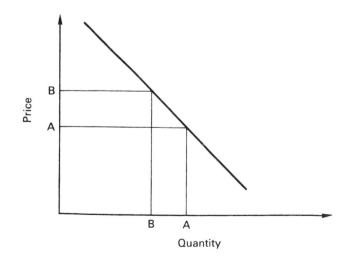

Figure 6.1 *The demand curve*

In this graph, you can see that a change in the price of the product will result in a comparable change in the quantity sold. If the demand curve is drawn at a shallower angle, like the one in Figure 6.2, you will see that a small increase in the price will result in a large change in the quantity sold. This indicates that the demand for the product is elastic.

However, if you make the curve into a steeply angled line, you will see that a large change in price will result in a small change in the quantity sold. This is called inelastic demand (Figure 6.3).

Inelastic demand tends to occur where there are no or very few substitutes for the product you are selling. This is because those

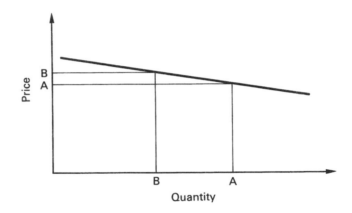

Figure 6.2 *The demand curve showing elastic demand*

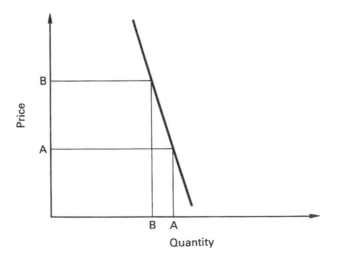

Figure 6.3 *The demand curve showing inelastic demand*

customers who have to buy or feel they need to buy the product will continue to buy despite the change in price. However, if there are substitutes for your product and you make a large increase in price, your customers may buy the substitutes. This effect can be seen in a number of markets. For example, the first microwave ovens were expensive, almost novelty, technology items. However, as more and more manufacturers produced them, their prices dropped and the market for them expanded. The demand moved from being inelastic to elastic. An even better example occurs every year as fresh fruit and vegetables appear in the markets. The earliest crops tend to be expensive and purchased for special occasions but, as more and more appear in the markets or shops, the price drops and more people buy them.

The same principle can be applied to the growing use of external suppliers to take over internal functions in both the public and private sectors – contract cleaning, contract catering, the use of agencies to handle specialized marketing functions, contract refuse disposal services. A number of benefits are claimed for this change:

- Better value for money.
- Lower costs.
- Accountable service.
- Allows the organization to concentrate on its core business.
- Reduces headcount or allows the organization to make more effective use of its existing people.

Whatever the benefit, this change demonstrates a change from inelastic demand for the internal service to elastic demand in the face of competitive action.

To summarize:

- A change in price has a **major effect** on sales when demand is **elastic**.
- A change in price has **little effect** on sales when the demand is **inelastic**.

Life cycles and price

The elasticity of demand changes over the life of a product or service. Many new products enjoy high prices in the introductory stage. As the product enters the growth phase, competitors offer the possibility of substitution. However, it may not be until maturity is reached that the effects of competition ensure demand proves to be elastic. In the later stages of saturation and decline you can expect demand to remain elastic and prices to reflect this. Price cutting and pricing strategies will be designed to win small but important market share from competitors.

Pricing and positioning

The benefits and the unique selling propositions you identified may justify a higher price for your products or services. If you can communicate these to your customers effectively, you will be able to justify higher prices and meet customers' expectations. Price may be a major determinant in the position and value of products or services in your market. Top of the range products or services may not be significantly better than others but what they have done is combine their positioning with their pricing.

Strategies for pricing products and services

Before you decide on a pricing strategy for your product or service, you need to ensure that the strategy is in line with overall corporate objectives.

New products or services

If a new product is the first of its kind, or significantly different or superior to existing products, demand could be inelastic and you might be tempted to adopt a price skimming strategy. You would expect sales to be low to begin with and growth to be relatively small. By setting your price high, you will not significantly affect your sales and you will be able to 'skim' the high profits of at this stage. The customers who buy your product or service will be those who are attracted to new and unique products. However, as competitors enter the field, demand will become more elastic. You will need to reduce your price to recognize these changes and to ensure that you maintain your market share. Your competitors will follow and a new price range will be set.

A skimming strategy has important benefits:

- You can recover your costs quickly and help fund the high cost of the launch.
- You can also fund further research to ensure that you maintain your market lead.
- You can keep production levels low to begin with.
- As you begin to enjoy the economies of scale which come with larger production runs and increased production capacity you will be able to lower the prices and still maintain a reasonable profit level.

However, there are also problems:

- High profits may tempt competitors into the market quicker than you would like.

■ High prices may slow down market entry, giving competitors the opportunity to enter the market later with better and cheaper products.

When video cassette recorders (VCRs) first entered the UK market, it was possible to rent a new video recorder every year. You could shop around and get the best deal for the most sophisticated machine, rent it for six months to a year and then shop around for a better machine. Each time you did this the quality and range of features increased dramatically and it was cost effective to rent rather than buy. Now it is probably more cost effective to buy a new machine every two or three years, if you think that the improvements are worthwhile.

Modified products or services

Most new products are not unique in the strictest sense. They are versions of existing products with new and improved qualities or features. They may be aimed at specific market segments and sometimes they can be new or unique to that sector only.

You may be one of the players who is following a price skimming player or you may be entering an established market with a new version of existing products or services. In both cases, your objective will also be significantly different from the previous player:

■ You will want to establish your product or service quickly and effectively.
■ You will want to achieve a good share of the existing market and to do this you may enter the market at a price which is much lower than the rest of your competition.

This strategy is commonly known as penetration pricing. Once you have established your place in the market, you can then begin to raise your prices and enjoy increased profitability while meeting the customer's price-confidence levels. This strategy has a number of benefits:

■ Immediate economies of scale brought about by high production levels.
■ Low prices will be partially offset by the economies of scale.
■ Speedy capture of market share.
■ The low profit margins, high investment levels and high risk discourage competitors.

There are also disadvantages:

■ You are seen as the low-cost option and, if you have little else to offer your customers, you may never be able to recover.
■ You may take longer to reach that share of the market.
■ You may find yourself failing to reach sufficient levels of sales to make any profits.

■ You may overextend yourself, end up with unsold stock and no reserves to develop or produce improvements to your products or services.

Existing products or services

Pricing strategies can be just as important for existing products:

■ You may be forced into a price change.
■ You can use price as a competitive tool.
■ The market may give you little room to manoeuvre on price.

If you are market leader, you will find that the market tends to use your prices as a yardstick for the whole market. You will be able to dictate the price-confidence level in the minds of the customers and, if you decide to change your prices, the rest of the market will probably follow your lead. If you decide to increase your prices because of inflation or other external circumstances, your competitors may delay their changes until they can see what the market does. Market reactions may work against you, and your competitors may delay their rises further in order to capitalize on these reactions. However, if you lower your prices in order to capture further market share or simply to pass on the benefits of your reduced costs, the rest of the players are more likely to react quickly and lower their prices to the new level set by you.

Short-term pricing tactics

Pricing tactics can help you meet a short-term objective and there are a number of possible approaches:

■ Promotional pricing.
■ Price discounts and allowances.
■ Discriminatory.

Promotional pricing

Promotional pricing tactics are used to support a product or service for a specific period of time:

■ **Loss leaders** Offering your customers a particular product or service at a very low price to encourage them to buy other products or services at normal rates.
■ **Cash rebates** Rebates provide flexibility and are less costly than discounts. For example, you might offer your customers a rebate if they buy before a certain time, boosting sales or clearing stock quickly.

■ **Low interest financing** Schemes offering low-cost finance through lease/buy deals as well as zero- or low-interest credit deals.

Price discounts and allowances

Apparent or actual reductions in price are offered to the customer in return for specific action:

■ **Cash discounts** Discounts for paying in cash, especially where there is a cost to the seller when customers pay by cheque or credit card. Other cash discounts may be offered by the seller to account customers who settle their bills within a certain period. This includes graded discounts for prompt payments and surcharges for late payment.

■ **Quantity discounts** Customers are given discounts based on the size of their orders – either a set discount per order or discounts on cumulative purchases. An example of a consumer quantity discount is the frequent-flier club where customers who use a particular airline are awarded points based on the number of miles they travel. At various point totals, the customer can claim specific rewards such as air tickets to destinations.

■ **Trade discounts** Manufacturers give discounts to different trade channels for warehousing, wholesaling and distributing their products. The term also refers to discounts given to professionals such as builders, plumbers and electricians who place larger and more frequent orders.

■ **Seasonal discounts** Manufacturers offer discounts during the slack season to encourage retailers and large users to place orders earlier. This can even out the levels of demand between the high and low seasons.

■ **Allowances** The most common forms of allowances are trade-in allowances on cars and other consumer durables.

Discriminatory pricing tactics

Products or services are sold to different markets or market sectors at different prices:

■ **Customer/segment pricing** Different prices for the same product are offered to different groups, for example, admission at different rates for students or old age pensioners.

■ **Product form pricing** Several versions of the same product which have only minor differences, for example, vegetables in supermarkets sold 'loose' cost less than the same vegetables packed in a plastic bag.

■ **Location pricing** For example, theatres, where prices vary according to the different locations of seats despite the fact that it costs the theatre the same to provide any given seat.

Competence self-assessment

1 What value would you put on the product or service your department provides? How could you improve the value to your internal customers?

2 How do your organization's prices compare with those of your competitors? Are you offering better quality or is your cost base higher?

3 What are the main cost elements of the internal service you provide? How could you improve your cost base?

4 If you were marketing the internal service your department provides to external customers, would you adopt a low, medium or high pricing strategy? How would you justify your strategy?

5 Can you give an example of a product you have bought recently which represents inelastic demand? What do you think the price might have been if there were substitutes and demand was elastic?

6 Which of the following cars might adopt a pricing policy based on inelastic demand: Rolls Royce Silver Shadow, BMW 7 series, Saab 9000 series? Why could they do this?

7 If your department was faced with competition from low-cost external suppliers, how would you respond? If you were unable to achieve the lowest price, what added value could you demonstrate?

8 Looking at your organization's product range, have you got new products where you can adopt a skimming policy?

9 Is your organization a price leader or follower? Do you think there are opportunities to raise or lower prices? What other actions would you take to support the price changes?

10 If you were marketing your department's services to external customers, what promotional pricing tactics would you adopt to enter a new market or increase sales?

7 The manager as supplier and customer

Why this chapter is important

This chapter looks at the process of meeting customer needs from the point of view of both customer and supplier. It shows that we fulfil both roles, and this can help us to improve our performance as a provider of services. The chapter shows how we can improve our performance as customers by helping our suppliers to provide a better service. It also shows how we might consider alternative methods of providing our services, using intermediaries or choosing different distribution routes.

Upstream and downstream

We are all customers and suppliers in our private as well as our work lives. I tend to think of supplying and buying as two aspects of the same process – the main difference is where we stand in the chain of supply. A farmer, for example, is at the beginning of the chain of supply of food, but at the end of the chain of supply of fertilizers or farm equipment, and in the middle of the chain for, say, seed potatoes.

Another way of looking at supplying and buying is to consider the flow of goods and services: supply is concerned with flow downstream from source to final user, while purchase is an upstream process where you are concerned with the receipt of goods, supplies or services. The concept of the chain links these two processes so that each of us is concerned with both upstream and downstream activities.

In this chapter I will look at the processes involved in managing both the upstream and downstream activities and identify the important management issues.

Overview

The outline in Figure 7.1 shows the purchasing and supply processes running parallel to each other.

The processes

Establishing need/promotion, research and selling

One of the basic elements of the buying process is the establishment of need. Taking a simple example: you realize that you are thirsty. You

THE PROCESSES	
Buying	*Supplying*
Establishing need ⎱ Specification ⎰ Source identification Source assessment Negotiation Agreement Managing the relationship Need fulfilled Reviewing process	Promotion, research and selling activities Evaluating specification Clarifying needs Negotiation Agreement Delivering Assessing success Identifying further needs
THE CONCERNS	
Ensuring the RIGHT . . . Source Specification Quality Price Quantity Time Place	 Customer Specification Quality controls Profit Order size Processing and delivery Delivery/distribution

Figure 7.1 *Parallel view – supplier versus buyer processes and concerns*

have established that you have a need – you want something t
quench your thirst – all you need to do now is decide what t
drink.

The next example is more complex. A divisional manager requeste
an additional secretary for his department, but the request was turne
down. Instead, his staff were given word processors and training, an
his department's productivity rose. His initial request indicated
need, but he had expressed it in the wrong way. His staff wer
inefficient because they were using typewriters for detailed and ofte
repetitive work. His need was not another person to act as typewrite
fodder, it was to give the existing secretaries a better set of tools t
make their tasks easier and quicker.

If you are a supplier, your main task at this stage is to ensure tha
customers have access to the right level of information so that they ca
identify potential needs and you can plan new products or services t
satisfy them.

Specification/promotion, research and selling

We need to make our specifications as clear and as unambiguous a
possible so that the supplier can understand exactly what it is we nee
and provide a precise solution – a product or service designed t
satisfy the need exactly.

Taking the example of the word processors:

- Should they be dedicated word processors or personal computers (PCs) with word-processing software?
- What type of PC and what other applications could it handle?
- Should the word processors share printers or each have a printer of their own?
- Where should they be located and do they need to be networked?
- If the secretaries have word processors, should you not supply them to other potential users in the department?
- How should you plan training and manage the changeover from the old system to the new?
- What budget should be allocated to the whole project?

By answering these and other relevant questions, you can compile a specification which reflects your short- and long-term requirements for the product. This takes more effort than saying 'get them all word processors and make sure they are all properly trained', but it ensures that you have given full consideration to your requirements and do not waste money on the wrong solution.

If you are the supplier, you can help your customer develop a clear specification by providing:

- Consultancy.
- Advice and guidance.
- Product or service guides which explain the importance of different features.

Source identification/evaluating specification

The specification should do more than define what you want to buy, it should also define the supplier's characteristics. Taking the word processor specification, the supplier profile would cover:

- Technical performance.
- Range.
- Installation and maintenance services.
- Training.

Desk research should indicate a range of suppliers who meet the specification. Supplement that by discussions with colleagues, customers' professional institutes, computer journalists. When you have drawn up a shortlist, make contact and assess the response:

- Phone the supplier, outlining your requirements and ask for information.
- Check how quickly they respond.
- Take note of how they deal with your enquiry and eliminate companies who respond poorly or offer you information on products that don't match your specification.
- Check the reputation of the company and their corporate values. Are they seen as a progressive and reliable supplier?

If you are a supplier, the key tasks at this stage are:

- Make a positive impression on the potential customer.
- Ensure that you fully understand their requirements.
- Try to assess who your competitors might be.
- Tailor the information you provide to the buyer to demonstrate that your solution matches their specification exactly.
- Make sure that you are capable of delivering the solution you have promised.

Source assessment/clarifying needs

How you assess a supplier depends on the importance of your relationship with the supplier – what contribution could the supplier make to the success of your business and how essential are the products or services supplied? You would spend more time assessing a supplier of computers than a supplier of pencils because computers give your business a competitive edge, pencils are a commodity item.

The supplier assessment can be carried out in a number of ways:

- Visiting the supplier's premises.
- Interviewing their representatives.
- Analysing their documentation, correspondence and publicity materials.

You are trying to judge whether they are the sort of organization you want to deal with:

- What is their approach to business?
- Are their representatives helpful and professional?
- Do they listen and respond to your needs?
- Can you trust them and could you work with them?
- What is their technical capability?
- How do they propose to produce these goods or services which they claim they can supply?
- How skilled and experienced are their staff and how efficient are their production facilities?
- Talk to their suppliers to get an unbiased opinion on the supplier.

Remember to keep a record of this process because it will prove valuable when you next need to select a supplier and, as you continue to add to your records, you will be able to build a useful database on suppliers and potential suppliers which can further improve your selection process. The records should not stop once you have selected your supplier. The best way of managing a relationship with your supplier is to maintain continuous records of performance; this will help you to monitor progress and identify problems before they become too serious.

Vendor assessment is a simple but effective method of assessing supplier performance. Select the most important aspects of the service and decide how much importance you place on each one. Decide on a method for assessing the factors you intend to use. Taking the word processor example, they had been using one supplier regularly for their computers, word processors, printers and software. They had three variables which were particularly important:

1 Their maintenance and repair services: they had an agreement that they would respond to callouts within an hour with an engineer, that they would either carry out the repair or provide a replacement within half a working day of the call and repair the fault within two working days. This had been carefully negotiated in order to ensure that they would be able to minimize the effects of any problem.
2 Their product quality.
3 Their prices.

Service was their most important factor so it was awarded 50 per cent of the total, while quality and price were given 25 per cent each. Service was measured by the number of times the supplier failed to meet the agreed standards and five points were deducted each time they failed.

Quality was calculated by deducting five points each time they had to replace a product immediately after installation and three points for every piece of equipment which failed before its warranty had expired.

They measured price performance by calculating the price they expected to pay as a percentage of what was actually paid.

This is the analysis for a quarter:

- They had been let down on service four times.
- On quality, two items had failed immediately after they had been installed and one item had failed after two months of use.
- They had done reasonably well on price and the quoted total price for the quarter was 93 per cent of actual price.

The vendor assessment calculation was as follows:

Service (50%) − (100 − 20) = 40
Quality (25%) − (100 − 13) = 21.75
Price   (25%) − 93   = 23.25

Performance score   = 85

Performance was down on the previous quarters because of the poor score on service and this was discussed with the supplier before placing the word processing order. They were subsequently given notice that the purchaser might consider changing the supplier if they continued to let them down.

If you are a supplier, you can take a more positive and proactive role at the source assessment stage. For example, the specification may be clear and unambiguous, but the supplier has specialist knowledge and a different perspective and may feel that the solution could be more effective. The supplier might also identify flaws in the specification which might not be obvious or important to the buyer.

You are seeking to win business against your competitors and yet you feel you may be at a disadvantage if you speak the truth and present the customer with problems. Experience and knowledge tell you that you need to modify the specification before you reach the negotiating stage, but how do you introduce these modifications without either losing the business or offending the potential customer? This stage requires tact, respect and integrity. It may be better to lose the order, rather than attempt to provide something that you know would be unsatisfactory to the customer.

As you develop a working relationship with your customer, you will be able to make an increasing contribution to their business and get involved in the earlier specifying stages of future projects.

Negotiation/negotiation

The aim of negotiation is to achieve the best possible agreement with your potential supplier or customer. The agreement should enable you to meet your business objectives without leaving your new supplier or customer in a position of disadvantage or dissatisfaction. Ideally, both parties should be committed to the principles and details of the agreement – in other words, a win–win situation. If you are a tough negotiator and end up with all of the advantages, you will leave your new supplier or customer feeling uncertain and this will not result in an effective business relationship.

McCall and Warrington's book *Marketing by Agreement*[1] sets out a professional negotiating philosophy:

- Both parties have a right and obligation to determine the goals and objectives they wish to achieve in the transaction.
- One party's goals and objectives might result in cost or risk for the other party. Where this happens, the party facing the risks or costs has the right to limit or protect against them or to be given additional consideration for accepting them.
- Responsibilities, costs and risks should be discussed, understood and allocated in an honest and open business manner. Both sides should avoid efforts designed to foster or permit misunderstanding or deception.
- Honest mistakes and misunderstandings may occur in the negotiations. Where this happens, both parties should try to resolve them.
- The best contract accurately sets forth the mutual understanding of both parties on all relevant issues.
- A good contract must also recognize that one or both parties may fail to perform their obligations under the agreement. The contract should include clear standards of performance and remedies. This may also help reduce the chance of litigation.

We can add a number of other guidelines:

■ Prepare for the negotiation. There is nothing worse than being in a situation where the other person is better prepared, better informed and therefore more confident about what they want. Never put yourself in a position of disadvantage.
   – Make sure you have a full knowledge and understanding of the people and the organization you are dealing with.
   – Be aware of details of costs, prices, timings, quality levels expected, and have comparable data on these from other suppliers.
   – Have a clear idea of your alternatives.
■ Set clear and precise objectives for the negotiations, including:
   – Acceptable and unacceptable outcomes.
   – Maximum levels of success you think that you could achieve.
   – Areas where you feel you could agree a compromise without sacrificing your main objectives.
■ Decide on an agenda and a timetable for the meeting, and agree it with the other party.
■ Remember that you do not need to finalize the negotiations at that meeting.
   – If you are uncertain or unhappy about the agreement, stop.
   – If the negotiations go on for a long time, remember that it may be unwise to sign agreements at the end of that session. Fatigue can affect judgement.
■ Take notes of all the important points in the meeting and circulate them to all participants as quickly as possible. Speed, accuracy and clarity can improve relationships, generate confidence and engender professionalism in your associates, suppliers and customers.

McCall and Warrington[2] identify a number of key stages in negotiation, shown in Figure 7.2.

Fisher and Ury[3] have some useful advice on the right mental approach to negotiations:

■ Separate the people from the problem. Avoid reacting with phrases like 'This is totally unacceptable' and use a more flexible approach such as 'I am very concerned that we have different interpretations of that point – I would like to give you our interpretation now . . .'
■ Focus on interests, not positions. It is the combination of support and attack which is most effective in negotiation.
■ Introduce options for mutual gain. If neither party can get everything they want, try to find a compromise or a partial or contingent agreement instead.
■ Insist on objective criteria. Focus on principle, not pressure; look for objective criteria such as fair standards and procedures and avoid battles for dominance as these often produce unsatisfactory agreements.

Stage	Description
Pre-negotiation	Preparation
Distributive bargaining	Listen to your potential supplier or customer; find out their requirements and the important issues
Integrative bargaining	Resolve the main issues with the other party; win and make concessions where necessary
Decision and action	Reach an equitable and mutually satisfying conclusion to the negotiations; confirm the main points to avoid confusion and misunderstanding
Post negotiation	Ratify any agreements

Figure 7.2 *Negotiation stages*

Agreement/agreement

There are a number of situations where negotiation does not take place and where the informal supplier/customer relationship is not controlled by negotiation. However, informal relationships between customer and supplier are not an excuse for a reduction in service.

Managing the relationship/delivering

The outcome of an agreement is not simply the delivery and receipt of goods or services, it is the beginning or continuation of a relationship which has to be managed. Key clauses in an agreement can help you ensure that the terms of the agreement are met; they include:

- Details on how and when the agreement can be terminated.
- Trial periods which can be used to develop the relationship.

The level of importance and size of the relationship will also affect how it develops and will dictate the amount of time and effort that you and the other party are prepared to put into it. From the supplier's point of view, each customer may be a relatively small part of their overall business and may not warrant high levels of attention. Major customers, on the other hand, influence the prospects of the company and an investment in managing relationships provides long-term benefit.

Need fulfilled/assessing success

The important questions to ask at this stage include:

- Did it fulfil the customer's needs properly?
  - Monitor the performance of the product and ensure that it is achieving performance criteria.
  - Assess product quality.
- Does it help you develop the right long-term relationship with the customer?

Taking the example of the word processors, once the secretaries were proficient at using their new machines, they looked for more sophisticated performance. The suppliers were able to develop new applications and our relationship with them grew closer as a result of the cooperation. However, as our systems expanded, we found that our original supplier did not have the resources to meet our changing requirements.

Reviewing process/identifying further needs

In reviewing the supply processes or attempting to identify further needs, the purchaser must monitor what has been provided:

- Is there is a better way of satisfying needs?
  - Better systems or improved products or service from your existing supplier.
  - Change your supplier to make a significant improvement.
- Should you include your suppliers in the review process? This can be done through meetings or through exchange of information.

The supplier also needs to review the processes and make certain that they have provided the best possible solutions and that they are providing the customer with a complete service:

- Other services or products are supplied by competitors, but the supplier feels that they could provide a much better service.
- There may be other products or services which the supplier can provide, but of which the customer is not aware.

These customer/supplier reviews can be extremely valuable because both parties may spend many months or even years in a relationship without even exploring the possibilities of change or growth. This might be simply because of the lack of communication between the two parties, but it should be remedied because the change could be mutually beneficial.

The concerns

There are a number of concerns which influence any purchasing or supplying situation. They include:

- Source.
- Specification.
- Quality.
- Price.
- Quantity.
- Distribution.

The right source

There is little benefit in choosing a supplier who does not suit your needs. You may have done this through expedience or through a need to keep costs down, but there is no reason why you should continue with a supplier simply because they were the cheapest or the quickest. You should be concerned about the supplier's or customer's attitudes and values if you wish to continue the relationship with them.

The right specification

This was covered earlier, but the key points to remember are:

- Ensure that the specification is clear and unambiguous.
- Involve your suppliers in the specification process as early as possible; they may be able to make a contribution which saves money and improves the solution.

The right quality

Quality is discussed in detail in a later chapter. In this section, we will assess how quality issues affect the relationship between supplier and buyer:

- Product or service quality can be measured so that both parties can base their agreements on standards rather than vague intentions.
- Quality cannot be isolated from delivery. Poor quality goods delivered on time are as useless as quality goods delivered late.
- Quality is important throughout the supply chain, particularly if you are buying or selling components to be used in other products. Final quality is dependent on quality at every stage.

The right price

Price and profit are not necessarily monetary measures – they include other benefits which will vary in importance according to your overall objectives. In supply chains utilizing Just-In-Time techniques, the price that the customer pays includes the cost of commitment and involvement with the supplier as well as the physical cost of the product. The supplier provides more than the product: he provides flexibility, responsiveness and an exceptionally high level of quality. Both parties gain, but they exchange more than simply money.

The right quantity

Quantity is just as important as price, time and quality. Over-ordering can seriously affect your cost structure, while under-ordering can affect delivery to your customers. Accurate forecasting and stock control will help you to achieve the right balance.

The right distribution

The choice of distribution channel can affect relations between suppliers and buyers. There are a number of choices:

- The customer collects the goods or receives the service directly from the supplier.
- The supplier uses their own delivery system.
- The supplier uses agents, wholesalers or other intermediaries.

Distribution systems

This section is about the role distribution plays in the supplier/customer relationship. The choice of distribution channels is determined by a number of factors including:

- The nature of the products or services.
- The number, size and location of customers.
- The complexity and sophistication of the products.
- The expectations of your customers.

Any changes you make to your distribution may have an impact on the whole of your marketing and business activities. For example, if a mail order company wanted to move into retailing, it would need to make a major investment in training to develop retailing skills. It would also face other problems:

- Stock control, selling and customer service management will be different.
- They will have less control over the distribution function.
- Distribution-cost structure will vary to reflect rent and maintenance of premises, staff, stock.
- Customer expectations in a retail outlet are different from mail order.

Figure 7.3 is a simplified diagram of distribution channels; it suggests that there are three factors affecting your choice of channels:

1 The selection of your intermediaries.
2 The use of your intermediaries.
3 The support of your intermediaries.

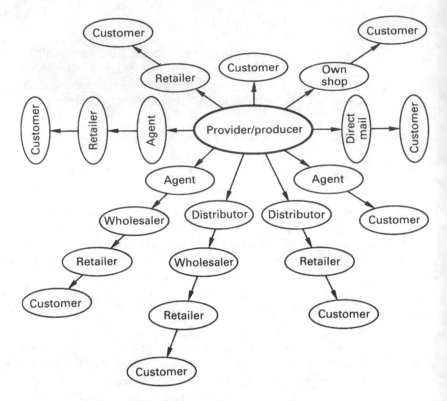

Figure 7.3 *Example of distribution channels*

The functions of the retailer are:

■ To buy in relatively large quantities from wholesalers or manu-facturers and to break these down into smaller quantities which are required by the individual customers.
■ To provide credit where appropriate.
■ To provide after-sales service where appropriate.
■ To advise the customer on quality, performance and specification.
■ To act as a liaison between the end customer and the manufacturer.
■ To prepare products for sale, for example, fresh produce such as vegetables, cheese or meat.

The functions of the wholesaler include:

■ To share financial risk by purchasing in advance of actual demand.
■ To stock products in convenient locations for the distribution process.
■ To break down bulk consignments from the manufacturer.
■ To provide a flow of information between retailers and the manufacturer.
■ To even out the fluctuations in supply, demand and price.

Control and distribution channels

Some organizations may start out owning and controlling the distribution process or may develop it over time. For example, Holiday Inn Hotels was a major customer to outside suppliers of carpets and furniture. Now, however, they have their own carpet mill and even their own furniture manufacturing plant. Virgin Records has developed from a record producer and distributor to a major retailer.

The issue of control is directly linked with the selection of the most appropriate channels and to the level of coverage you can achieve through the use of intermediaries. Figure 7.3 is a simplified diagram of the distribution channels open to you. The length of the arrow is an indication of the level of control and the cost. The shorter the arrow, the smaller the level of control you will retain over your products. The longer the arrow, the greater the costs of distribution.

Selecting distribution channels

Distribution strategy will depend on the following factors.

Markets and customers

- If you have a large number of customers who are widely scattered and who order frequently but in small quantities, it may be more practical to use a network of wholesalers or retailers to reach them.
- If you have a few customers who place high-value orders, it may be more profitable for you to deal with them directly.

Figure 7.4 summarizes the effects of the main customer/market factors on the length of the distribution channels you are likely to use.

	Conditions favouring	
Factors	**Long channels**	**Short channels**
1 Size of purchasing unit	Small	Large
2 Number of customers	Many	Few
3 Location of customers	Geographically dispersed	Geographically concentrated
4 Customer knowledge	Considerable and widely dispersed	Limited and concentrated
5 Installation and servicing assistance	None required	Help required

Figure 7.4 *Basic factors affecting channel length: customers/markets*

Products and services

The type of product or service you distribute will also help to determine your choice. The factors include:

- The type of product.
- Its uses.
- Its values.
- The amount you produce and the level of demand.
- Seasonality.
- Competition.
- Special attributes.

In industrial markets, it is more common for the manufacturer to have direct contact with the customer either because orders are large or because the products have to be specially designed to meet each customer's particular needs.

Fast-moving consumer goods need to be distributed so that they are easily accessible to the customer. Perishable goods also need to be distributed quickly and efficiently on a regular basis. In both cases, supermarkets must be able to keep their shelves stocked and manufacturers need to work closely with the retailers and wholesalers to ensure that fresh supplies are maintained.

Product characteristics can help you determine distribution channels and Figure 7.5 shows the factors affecting channel length for different products and services.

Company factors (Figure 7.6)

The key factors include:

- Size of your organization.
- Financial strength.
- Location.
- Level of control.
- Level of market information.
- Strength in the marketplace.

Competitive factors (Figure 7.7)

These include:

- The number of competitors.
- Your organization's strength in the market.
- Competitors' level of control or influence over the channels.
- Economic and legal factors affecting competition.

Distribution and marketing activities

Can you use a broader mix of distribution channels? By reviewing existing channels and considering other options, you may identify a number of other channels which might help widen your market or

Factors	Conditions favouring	
	Long channels	**Short channels**
1 Perishability	Low	High
2 Fashionability	Low	High
3 Size of product	Small	Large
4 Value of product	Low	High
5 Weight of product	Light	Heavy
6 Complexity of product	Technically simple	Technically complex
a Special knowledge for sale	None	Considerable
b Installation	Not necessary	Required
c Maintenance	Not required	Frequent or regular
d Service	Not required	Frequent or regular
7 Risk of obsolescence	Low	High
8 Age of product	Old	New
9 Production process	Standard	Custom built
10 Order size (quantities purchased)	Small	Large
11 Appearance of product	Undifferentiated (homogeneous)	Differentiated (heterogeneous)
12 Type of product (buying characteristics)	Convenience good	Speciality good
13 Type of product (market)	Consumer good	Industry good
14 Time of purchase	Seasonal	Non-seasonal
15 Timing of purchase	Frequent	Infrequent
16 Regularity of purchase	Regular	Irregular
17 Profit margin	Low	High
18 Width of product line	Narrow	Broad
19 Availability requirements	Delayed	Immediate
20 Number of products per line	Few	Many
21 Product lines	Unrelated	Related
22 Number of alternative uses	Many	Limited

Figure 7.5 *Basic factors affecting channel length: products/services*

Factors	Conditions favouring	
	Long channels	**Short channels**
1 Size of firm	Small	Large
2 Length of time in business	New to market	Old and established in the market
3 Financial resources	Limited	Abundant
4 Location in the market	Not centrally located	Centrally located
5 Control over marketing programme	Unimportant	Important
6 Overall resource position	Weak	Strong
7 Market coverage desired	Intensive	Exclusive
8 Managerial capabilities	Weak	Strong
9 Market information availability	Limited	Abundant and expensive
10 Power	Weak	Strong
11 Policy toward pushing product	Passive	Aggressive

Figure 7.6 *Basic factors affecting channel length: company/organization*

Factors	Conditions favouring	
	Long channels	**Short channels**
1 Number of competitors	Many	Few
2 Number of resources controlled	Few	Many
3 Economic conditions	Recessionary	Booming
4 Entry and exit of producers	Easy	Limited
5 Economic customs and traditions	Stable	Dynamic
6 Location of competitors	Geographically dispersed	Geographically concentrated
7 Laws and regulations	Tight	Loose
8 Competition among customers	Weak	Strong
9 Market to be served	New	Old

Figure 7.7 *Basic factors affecting channel length: competition/external*

help you reach a specific market segment better. Some examples show the possibilities:

- The Post Office significantly expanded the purchase of postage stamps by allowing them to be sold in other retail outlets instead of exclusively through their own post office and sub-post office network.
- The increased use of mail order catalogues by upmarket retailers such as Harrods. Their aim was not to lure customers away from their own store but rather to capture new customers who either did not live near their store or who were too busy to spend much time shopping but still aspired to buying their goods. By selling through their catalogue, they opened up new market opportunities.

You can have a profound influence on the way in which your distribution channels perform by deciding whether to 'push' or 'pull' your product or service through them:

- You can 'pull' the product or service through the channel by concentrating on the end consumers and by using various promotional techniques.
- You can 'push' it through by concentrating on gaining the cooperation of intermediaries. This can be achieved by providing incentives, exerting pressure through your relationship with them and demonstrating your support for the intermediary.

Dealing with intermediaries

These are some of the advantages of using intermediaries:

- They enable you to keep in touch with the many outlets that may stock or want to stock your product.
- They can act as a buying agent for the retailer and a sales agent for the producer.
- You can minimize your own stock holding where the intermediary holds stock for you.
- They can take on some of the risk by holding stock which may suffer damage, deterioration.
- They may have greater expertise than you in selling to the markets you want to reach.
- They can reduce the cost of reaching the final customer by saving you the cost of maintaining a field salesforce.
- By buying in bulk they can relieve you of the high cost of handling large numbers of small orders.
- They can provide a local point of sale.

The disadvantages include the following:

- The way the product reaches and is presented to the final customer may be out of your direct control.

- Reduced profit margins as every level of intermediary requires a percentage share of the profits. However, this may still prove cheaper than setting up your own distribution network.
- You might be tempted to spend more time trying to understand and please those in the distribution channels than you do on your customers.

There is a trade-off and you must decide the relative importance and value of each advantage and disadvantage before you select your channels.

Terms and conditions

There are specific concerns and issues which you need to address before entering into an agreement with an intermediary. These include the following key areas:

- What trade margins, discounts and credit are you prepared to offer? These help push the product through the channel and must be carefully negotiated to ensure that the distributor is satisfied, that they are not going to disadvantage you in relation to your competitors and that they are within your own accepted limits.
- Are the agreed delivery times acceptable and achievable? You should never promise the impossible and always keep to the delivery dates and times you agreed.
- Do not forget to agree quality standards. You should always discuss quality with new distributors and share your commitment to quality with them.
- It is in both your interests to agree minimum order sizes. These must be carefully calculated and reviewed as business increases and develops.
- Be aware of territories and market share deals. Remember that your distributors will have competitors too and so it may be to both your advantages to agree exclusive distribution rights with individual distributors in specific marketing areas or territories. The size of the territories will also determine the potential size of orders secured from the distributors.
- Provide the right level of promotional support. Most distributors want to see the products being 'pulled' through the system with the help of advertising, sales promotion, and other forms of support. Try to keep your distributor up to date and properly informed about your promotional activities so that they can forecast changes in demand and support your products.
- Don't forget aftercare, complaints handling and other related activities. You can provide training to the distributor's staff and, where necessary, deal with complaints, and provide repair and maintenance service to enhance the level of aftercare to the customer.

Distributing a service

Services are not physical objects, but any service provider from a hairdresser to a management consultant still has distribution decisions to make. These decisions include the following:

- Where should it be delivered? Should you go to the customer or should the customer come to you, should your transactions be carried out on the street, by post, over the telephone, in the customer's home or office or in your own home or office? There is a trend towards more and more services being provided using computers and telephone line links.
- How should you deliver your service? Should you offer your customers a choice in the way in which it is to be delivered? Banks and building societies now offer a number of different forms of delivery for the same service, ranging from on-line telephone links to your own computer, a variety of different cash dispensing and service machines, personal telephone service, postal and counter services.
- Should you use an agent or some other intermediary to provide your services? Most insurance companies use a wide range of agents some of whom are directly employed by the company while others work on a commission-based system and may have similar contracts with other insurance companies.
- Can you use different distribution channels to help you segment or to serve different segments which already exist? For example, you might plan to use your distribution channels as part of your marketing strategy with different market segments being offered the service via different channels.
- Does one channel provide you with additional competitive advantage?
- Does a channel add to your service or allow additional services to be provided which could not otherwise be provided to your customers? For example, providing a cable TV service may be your primary business but once you have laid the cables and attracted subscribers you can then provide telephone services, other cable-based interactive services, test marketing and other facilities through one distribution channel.

Distribution in internal markets

Internal markets have their own distribution channels. We all have customers and suppliers and we are part of a chain of supply from originators to end users. We all need to rely on colleagues for part of the delivery of our products or services and these indirect links are part of the distribution channel within the internal market.

Stockholding, quantities and JIT

There are two basic approaches to controlling inventories and managing stock levels:

1 Fixed order quantity.
2 Fixed interval.

Figures 7.8 and 7.9 illustrate what happens to stock over time when the two approaches are applied.

In the fixed order quantity approach, there is a fixed time between

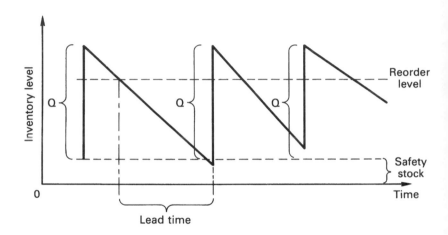

Figure 7.8 *The effect on stock of the fixed order quantity approach*

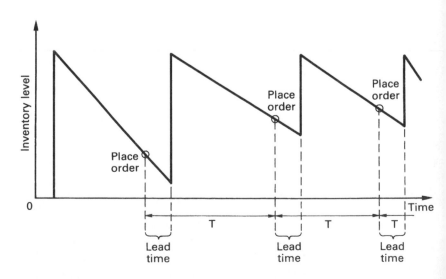

Figure 7.9 *The effect on stock of the fixed interval approach*

ordering stock and its delivery so you need to ensure that this does not affect your stock detrimentally.

■ Calculate the amount of stock you would use between ordering new stock and its delivery.
■ Add on the quantity of stock you intend to use as a buffer in case of delay in delivery.
■ Add these two quantities together, to calculate the reorder level.
■ Calculate a fixed amount of stock which should be ordered each time stock levels reach the reorder level.

The time between placing and receiving an order is known as the lead time. In the figure you can see that the maximum amount of stock available tends to be relatively constant and that the stock level seldom eats into the safety or buffer stock.

In the fixed internal approach, there is a fixed time between orders.

■ The amount that you order will vary according to the rate of use of stock and the amount which needs to be ordered to replenish the stocks.
■ If the original stock is used up rapidly, you will need to order a large quantity.
■ If the rate of usage drops, the amount you will need to order will consequently be lower.

Just-In-Time

Just-In-Time or JIT aims to remove the problems of stock control by reducing stock levels to the absolute minimum. The relationship with the supplier and the process of manufacturing supplies as they are required reduces uncertainties in supply. This closer relationship with the supplier also improves quality control because JIT aims for total quality from supplier through to finished product. It is clear that the customer gains a great deal from this approach. Suppliers gain a long-term commitment and closer working relationship with the customer.

Competence self-assessment

1   Can you identify the upstream and downstream links in the supply chain within your organization? Where do you stand in the chain?

2   Where does your organization stand in the supply chain? Identify your organization's key suppliers.

3 You are buying a new filing system for your department. Discuss whether you will buy a conventional system or move to computerized information handling. Prepare a specification for your new system.

4 What is your procedure for handling enquiries coming into your department? How could you improve the process?

5 Outline a vender assessment system for one of your most important suppliers. Include key factors and measurements.

6 You have identified a number of recurring problems with an important supplier, but you wish to continue working with them. Outline your key objectives for a performance review meeting with the supplier.

7 What improvements would you like your most important suppliers to make and how could you help achieve them?

8 How does your organization currently distribute its products and services? What other channels could it utilize?

9 What actions would be needed to support the new distribution channels? What risks are involved in using these new channels?

10 What is your organization's relationship with its main distributors? What forms of support could you provide to improve the performance of the distributor network?

11 How could you incorporate the Just-In-Time philosophy into the work of your department?

References

1 McCall, J. B. and Warrington, M. B. (eds) (1989) *Marketing by Agreement* (2nd edn), John Wiley, New York.
2 McCall, J. B. and Warrington, M. B. *op. cit.*
3 Fisher, R. and Ury, W. (1983) *Getting to Yes: Negotiating Agreement Without Giving In*, Hutchinson, London.

8 Dialogue with your customers

Why this chapter is important

Dialogue enables us to communicate information to our customers and get feedback from them so that we can help them make informed purchasing decisions in our favour. This chapter explains the different types of internal and external communications techniques and explains how to select and use the most appropriate technique. It will help make your communications more effective by showing you how to develop an understanding of what your audience needs to know to make a purchasing decision.

The importance of dialogue?

Most management books use the word 'communication' when discussing the processes of advertising, public relations, sales aids, sales promotion, and so on. I have given this chapter a title which emphasizes the word 'dialogue' because this is what I believe we should be striving to do when we plan our communications. It is, I believe, too easy to ignore the fact that communication is a two-way process – putting across a message and receiving a reply. If you are concerned with quality and with meeting your customers' needs effectively, you must understand and utilize communications effectively and creatively.

We need to have dialogue for these reasons:

- We need to inform others and know that they understand what we are saying to them.
- We need to influence others and know that they have been influenced in the way we wanted them to be.
- We need to win support or commitment and know that this is what they are giving us.
- We need to identify and promote our Unique Selling Points (USPs) and get our customers to tell us if they meet their requirements and what needs to be changed or improved.
- We need to let our customers know that we listen to them.
- We need to develop the identity of our products, services or brands and know that this identity is recognized and is shared with our customers.
- We need to communicate our improvements and be sure that they have been recognized and that we are on the right track.

- We need to develop esteem within our internal markets and know that this is shared (that people are 'proud to be part of the team').
- We need to build networks which provide internal and external support for our communications.
- We need to motivate staff internally and get positive feedback.
- We need to share our vision with staff and colleagues and win their support and commitment.
- We need to win trust and know that the trust is there.

The elements of dialogue

Dialogue is part of the relationship between supplier and customer and should be continuous. Unfortunately, many organizations only have true dialogue with customers when there are problems or complaints.

Even in the simplest models of communication such as the one illustrated in Figure 8.1, the emphasis is on the communication of the message rather than the process of dialogue.

- The sender identifies the target audience, a message is formulated and transmitted through a medium to the audience.
- The message is an imperfect tool of communication, so the sender has to invest a great deal of time, money, energy and expertise in getting the message to be as clear as possible.
- The medium used to carry the message is also carefully selected in order to reach the audience in their most receptive state.
- The message needs to be encoded to send it through the medium; the audience has to decode it to understand it.
- Between the sender and the audience and around the medium can be found noise which distorts and detracts from the message.
- The dotted line shows the potential for response and feedback.

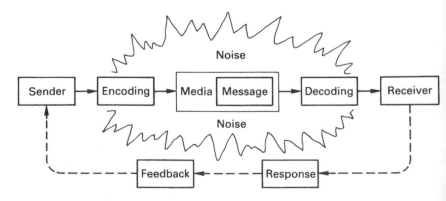

Figure 8.1 *Simplified model of communication processes*

The factors which affect dialogue include:

- Who do you want to communicate with and at what level?
- What do you want to communicate?
- What response do you want?
- Which media should you communicate through?
- How effective was the communication?

These factors operate within a wide range of constraints and are influenced by a number of circumstances. Let us look at how the factors will be affected within the three broad contexts I have used through this book:

1 The consumer market.
2 The business to business market.
3 The internal market.

Look carefully for the similarities and consider how the contexts change the way in which each factor is approached.

The consumer market

Communications is central to marketing a consumer product successfully. Let us take the example of marketing a snack food in Britain. In formulating a plan for communication you will need to use all of the data and information collected since the product's launch. You will have research data, market reports, advertising analyses and sales figures to help you. You will also work with advertising, research and other specialist agencies.

Let us look at the factors in this context.

Who and at what level?

The 'who' will be defined by market research, refined by other research and market analyses. You will have a number of segmentation alternatives for your market and a lot of information on how, why, where and when your products are bought and consumed. You will also know about competitors' products and how much the overlap is between your markets. Communication will need to be at several levels according to your market. For example, you might need to:

- Establish and maintain your brand image and keep it in the minds of actual and potential customers (e.g. by advertising in a teenage magazine).
- Support the consumption behaviour patterns of your consumers (e.g. school break consumption, cinema consumption, etc.).
- Support the product at point of sale by reaching purchasers and supporting retailers and wholesalers (e.g. by providing attractive point of sale).

What do you want to communicate?

You will know the product's USPs and research will have explained to you useful aspects of your product's image, patterns of consumption, types of people who consume, etc. You will use these to formulate your messages to each segment at each level. However, the messages must be consistent across all communications and at all levels. You will wish to avoid creating disappointment or creating confusion – the message must be compatible with the product as well as consistent at all levels.

What response do you want?

At the branding and image level you will wish to create a certain feeling about and image for your product in the customer's mind. The response you will be seeking is for the market to be more predisposed to buy your brand over and above other brands. You will use this branding to help you target segments who relate consuming your brand to leisure and other activities. You will be looking for regular purchase of your brand as well as seeking new customers who have switched to you from your competitors. You might also be looking for information on customers through the use of coupons and other response mechanisms.

Which media?

You will need to use a variety of media. Branding and other image communications will be targeted across the whole of your market and will use most of the broadcast media (TV, press, etc.). Specialist publications, cinema advertisements and posters strategically located may be employed to help re-enforce consumption patterns, as might sponsorship of sports, etc. Trade press and sales representative activity will help you push the brand through the distribution chain. Coupons, local advertisements, leaflets and point-of-sales support will all help at the purchasing stage.

How effective was it?

You will need to use research and sales data to help you assess your success. Some informal research will help you monitor the progress of your communications activities – especially if the research and sales data is expected to take a long time to produce. Any form of reliable monitoring during the process will help you to avoid disasters and capitalize on exceptional successes.

The business to business market

Consider the office equipment supplier who was marketing PCs to the company in the previous chapter. If you were responsible for communications within that organization what would you need to think about?

Who and at what level?

Knowledge of your market and the buyer behaviour which dominates it would be essential. Research would tell you who:

- Buys.
- Influences the decision.
- Selects suppliers.
- Makes the purchasing decisions.
- Places the order.
- Pays for the goods/services.
- Evaluates the purchase.

The number of important members of the decision process will vary according to the size and type of organization. Who you wish to communicate with will be determined by this knowledge and by the objectives of the communications. You will need to use the communications to do different tasks at each level in the buying process. Knowing what each player is ultimately seeking is essential.

What do you want to communicate?

There is likely to be more than one message. It will depend on the sector you are targeting. However, it will be necessary to separate out the functions of different types of communication – one communication containing different types of message seldom works. Thus, prestige, stability and success may impress the senior managers who need to approve the purchase but technical ability and quality are more likely to impress the technician who selects suppliers in the first place, etc. So, general branding advertising may appeal to all levels but specific messages may need to be put across to different players in the buying process.

What response do you want?

There may be many individuals to communicate with potentially, but what you want is for your organization to be the preferred supplier who gets most, if not all, of the relevant business and continues to get the business despite competitor activities. You want a profitable long-term relationship with your customers.

Which media?

You may use specialist press and special sections of the national press as media for branding and image building. Local radio and selective posters might also be useful. Detailed messages can be carried in some specialist press and details presented through public relations work may be used. Direct mail will be a very useful medium helping you to put across selective messages to different groups and with as much detail as required. Trade fairs and directories will keep your company visible and available while your sales representatives keep existing customers and find new ones.

How effective was it?

If you have a sales team and have staff dealing regularly with specific customers you will be able to monitor the progress of any communications efforts on a daily and weekly basis. You may need to supplement this with research and analyses of your sales/orders figures. You will be able to evaluate each element of the communications mix during the process as well as after it, thus averting major disasters and capitalizing on major successes as they arise.

The internal market

In this case, you and your department have been working on a set of quality improvements which are important to your department but could (ultimately) affect all of the other departments in your organization. This is your initiative and although tentatively supportive, the senior management have left it to you to sell the changes to the rest of the organization.

Who and at what level?

You and your team have worked out who the decision makers are, who the implementing officers will be and which actual workers will be affected by the changes you are proposing. It is also clear that you need to keep the senior managers directly and indirectly informed of your progress.

You will need to communicate formally and informally with each group in each department.

What do you want to communicate?

You should not try to communicate a *fait accomplis* in this situation!

Staff must be involved in the changes which affect them. Their input to the changes will be vital to win their support as well as improve the final process and make it work properly.

What you need to communicate are the benefits of the changes. Next you need to communicate your willingness to involve staff in the changes and the importance of their involvement. Finally you need to show them how to be involved and make it happen. You want the senior managers to see that your changes have the support and enthusiasm of the other departments.

What response do you want?

You want commitment and involvement and ultimately you want change. You also want recognition, support and commitment from senior management.

Which media?

Letters, memos and reports play a small but important part of the whole. Meetings, phone calls, presentations, discussions, lunches and drinks after work, discussion papers and forums, copies of magazine articles and reports which inspired you to make the changes, and even visits from people in other organizations who have tried similar approaches, are all ways of carrying your message to your audience. You need to work with your department as a team and you need to target potential advocates in key departments and enlist their aid too.

Senior managers need to hear of your success through sources in other departments as well as from you personally.

How effective was it?

You and your staff need to be monitoring and reviewing progress continuously and making changes/adjustments whenever necessary. This monitoring process will help you refine and develop each department's ultimate involvement in your quality improvement process as well as indicate where new advocates are appearing and pockets of resistance are holding out.

Summary

These examples illustrate the common strands as well as the differences between each context. There are essential elements in the communications process which always have to be addressed. Earlier chapters in this book have provided a considerable grounding which will help you address these elements. They include:

- Understanding your customers fully.
- Understanding the buying processes.
- Segmenting your markets properly.

- Understanding your products/services fully.
- Having clear objectives for your communications.
- Translating objectives and understanding into messages.
- Understanding costs and the role of pricing.
- Getting your timing right.
- Understanding what the media can do.
- Understanding your competition.
- Establishing feedback routes and listening to your customers.

In the rest of this chapter I will look at those elements not alread
covered in earlier chapters. I will also look at the planning processe
which will help you deal with communications more effectively.

Understanding advertising

Advertising has a number of elements. It contains:

- A message and some information for the audience.
- A catalyst or trigger to help put the message across (e.g. emotion
  excitement, beauty, youth, music, colour, endorsement, etc.).
- The authority of a medium.
- Emphasis of the benefits attached to the product/service.
- Association with specific images or events.
- The price.
- Availability.
- Links with other products or services.
- Customer service and other benefits.

Of course, there is a wide range of theories on how advertising
works. They add to our perspective but are not universal laws.

Some advertising theories/models

Let us look at some general theories of how advertising works whic
are often referred to in discussions.

AIDA – this is not only an opera by Verdi, it is also a model of how
advertising works. The letters stand for

Awareness > Interest > Desire > Action

This is rather simple compared to the huge systems models fo
buyer behaviour but the process behind each word can be just a
complex. Part of the reason for its simplicity is that it was firs
proposed in the 1920s and, although it points to the effects which yo
need to consider in the advertising process, it omits all of th
influences which exist in the buyer behaviour models. It says you nee
to get your advertising seen by prospective buyers, the advertisin
must then be read and believed in order for interest to be generate

and for desire to be created in the customer's mind. When these have been successfully achieved the outcome is the purchase of your product or service. It supports the idea that advertising persuades people to buy but demonstrates that the process is not simple.

A more recent model of the same sequential type was suggested by Colley in 1961[1] where he proposed the process which involved 'Defining Advertising Goals for Measured Advertising Results'. This was given the mnemonic DAGMAR. It takes things a bit further by pointing out that you need to have a clear goal or set of goals in mind before you begin the advertising process. It also recognizes that the results should be measurable.

The sequence is as follows:

- The customers start off unaware of your product or service.
- Advertising moves them through awareness to comprehension.
- From comprehension you win a conviction from customers (make them 'predisposed to buy').
- The advertising then encourages them to buy.

The idea of there being a sequence of events which make advertising work is a nice one but it does not fit with known experience of how people buy and it simplifies a process which is too complicated even for buyer behaviour models to explain satisfactorily.

Another sequential model is ATR which stands for Awareness, Trial and Reinforcement. It suggests that advertising's purpose is to encourage trial of the product or service and then reinforce the experience of the product in order for repurchase to take place. It recognizes the part which outside influences have in the process. In the first stage of the sequence the individual's awareness is focused on the brand. Trial may take place after this or a period where discussion and information from other sources about the brand will add to the reasons for trial purchase. Once bought, the purchaser is then reassured by the advertising.

The beauty of the models is that you can find examples of each at work every day. They are simple enough to add to our understanding without having to bind us to one model for every situation.

The simple models are supplemented by a number of complex studies of the effects of advertising which seek to identify and quantify the effects which can be attributed to advertising itself. They can produce excellent results but they do not explain how advertising works, only evaluate and predict its effects when it works.

The theories surrounding USPs and brands themselves can help us by adding further to our view. I have discussed USPs earlier and have suggested in this chapter that part of the input to an advertisement will be your product or service's USP. Reeves[2] suggests that our customers tend to remember only one thing from an advertisement. What he calls 'one strong claim or one strong concept'. By using this to bring your product or service's USP to the customers you should be able to make your advertising more effective.

So, what are BRANDS? Brands do the following:

- Give products or services an individual identity.
- Give a legal identity to products/services.
- Give them an identity in the eyes of customers.
- Promote attributes which distinguish your brand from others.
- Enable these attributes to live through product/service changes.
- Maintain part of the relationship with customers.
- Define expectations of quality and consistency which you seek to promote.

Each brand comes from your investment in it and this image, these attributes, can be passed on to other products or services which share it. An example of this is the Mars Ice Cream bar, which builds on the success of the chocolate bar of the same name. Branding also helps manufacturers to maintain and develop their product portfolios and allows them to let old products be replaced with new ones while maintaining their brand share of the market.

Advertising media – vehicles for communication

A medium is something which carries a message. The plural of medium is media. In the circles where advertising is studied, where there are a number of media sharing the same major characteristics (for example, the quality Sunday newspapers) each individual in the media group is referred to as a vehicle (something which also carries messages). So *The Sunday Times* and *The Observer* are known as vehicles in the generic media group the quality Sunday newspapers.

Figure 8.2 shows a simple way of looking at the whole spectrum of media which can be used in your communications plans. Think of a media group or medium and see if you can place it within the matrix. I have included some media groups or types to help you. When you are making your communications plans you will need to consider the nature of the media available to you, their characteristics and uses. This matrix is a good starting point.

In addition to these characteristics you will have to consider the following:

- The cost of using the medium.
- How well it reaches your chosen target groups.
- The cost effectiveness of using the medium.
- The authority and environment provided by the medium itself.
- The type of message best carried by the medium.
- The medium's ability to produce the response you want.
- The number of times people will get the message through the medium.
- The timing of the medium and its delivery of the message.
- The other messages, if any, carried by the medium.

	Broadcast		Narrowcast
Carries no advertising	Public broadcast media (BBC radio or TV)	Local public radio stations	Personal communication
Mixture	National press Commercial TV	Local press Local commercial Radio Cable TV	Trade and specialized press
Carries only advertising	Posters	Trade fairs Home shopping TV	Salesforce Direct mail Telephone sales

Figure 8.2 *Matrix of media categories*

■ The relationship your product/service might have with the medium.

If any of these characteristics take precedence in your considerations you may wish to create your own matrix with, for example, cost effectiveness in reaching your target audience as the x axis and perceived degree of authority or relevance on the y axis. With so many things to consider it will be useful to review very briefly the main media available to you.

Television

Television is mainly a broadcast medium. In the UK there is public service broadcasting (via the BBC) and commercial TV. In addition to the two terrestrially broadcast commercial stations (ITV and Channel 4) there are satellite TV stations, a number of cable TV companies and some 'stations within stations' such as the scrambled TV signal broadcast by the BBC for a subscription viewing company.

Over 98 per cent of homes in the UK have TVs and over 50 per cent have two or more.

TV advertising allows simple, strong messages to be presented with the full use of colour, movement and sound. Advertisers can pay for advertising slots alongside programmes compatible with their products/services. Its use for branding and image building is prodigious, fast moving consumer goods (FMCG) such as instant coffee can be advertised most effectively. Certain groups are difficult to reach through TV and where messages are very complex or markets are very small and dispersed, TV may be inappropriate.

Cost of advertising space and production can be very high but this can be offset by being able to reach large numbers of target audience very effectively and the cost per thousand homes reached can be very much smaller than for any other medium.

Press

This is the largest and most varied class of media available. The media in this group includes broadcast through to very narrowcast vehicles. In the UK this includes the following range:

National press including –

- Daily newspapers.
- Weekend newspapers and colour supplements.
- Weekly magazines including a wide range of women's and specialist interest magazines.
- Biweekly and monthly magazines.
- Other specialist trade/professional journals and papers.
- Directories.

Then there are regional and local publications including –

- Daily and weekly regional newspapers.
- Daily and weekly local papers.
- Free newspapers and other free publications.
- Local and regional directories.

Finally, there are restricted circulation publications bought on subscription only. These include professional and society/club publications and catalogues.

It is difficult to make general statements on such a variety of advertising and communications opportunities. However, most publications which offer advertising will be able to provide you with rates for different sized advertisements and will be able to tell you, on average, how many copies of their publication are sold or distributed. Many will be able to provide research data regarding the number and types of readers who look at their publications. From this data you will be able to calculate how much it will cost per thousand readers to reach your selected audience. As many readers will read more than one publication, research and analysis may be able to tell you what the overlap will be and identify the most efficient ways of using combinations of publications. An advertising agency or media specialist may be needed to help you perform this task.

Each publication has its own character and authority, and there may be opportunities to place your advertising in suitable positions within publications, thus taking advantage of the special authority which that position offers. For example, home improvement products may benefit from being placed on or adjacent to the home improvement page of a newspaper. Specialist publications also provide important opportunities for advertisers operating in that field of specialization.

Production costs can be very flexible, as can the lead time from deciding to advertise and advertising. Frequency of advertising and timing must also be carefully considered. Monthly magazines may remain in a reader's home for some time, while daily newspapers will usually have a very short life-span. So, the number of advertisements placed, the issue you place advertisements in and the job you expect the advertisement to do will all have to be carefully thought through. Press can also provide you with an effective response mechanism (reply/tear off slip, etc.).

Direct mail

In terms of both revenue and volume, direct mail is the third largest medium in the UK. Direct mail is frequently confused with unaddressed leaflets and other advertising posted through the letterbox. Direct mail can be defined as promotional material personally addressed to individuals and sent through the postal system to homes or places of work.

This medium is both highly targeted (narrowcast) and carries nothing but the message you have designed for it. This gives you a number of opportunities and responsibilities.

The message can be as short or as long as you wish and can be as complicated or simple as it needs to be. It goes only to those you have decided it should go to. However, these two facts require that you need to be absolutely certain of who you are sending the direct mail shot to and that the message is appropriate and relevant to the recipients. The power of the medium may backfire on you if your targeting is poor or your message is not appropriate.

The cost of direct mail is often regarded as relatively high but with proper targeting you pay to reach only those you wish to reach. Furthermore, it is an extremely powerful communication tool.

The medium's cost is in three basic parts:

- Production costs – design and copy writing, printing, folding and stuffing in envelopes.
- Address list costs – identifying, selecting and renting lists of names and addresses.
- Postage costs – postage rates can be reduced through a series of discounts for bulk, presorting and so on.

The medium is also extremely flexible. You can test a variety of creative and copy approaches, test a variety of lists and vary numbers sent, timings of mailings, and so on. Response opportunities are also considerable with this medium and mailings to existing and past customers can use and build on existing or past relations to develop a full dialogue with those customers.

Radio

This is an expanding medium with a number of new national as well as regional stations to choose from. Although basically a broadcast medium, the new stations attempt to serve particular niches within society and this means improved targeting for those attempting to reach these sub-groups of society. Recent examples include Jazz FM and Classic FM. Local radio stations serve niches through selective programming and this enables local advertisers to choose particular time slots on radio to maximize their communications efforts. It is also possible (but not always easy) to place the same advertisement on a number of local stations across the country. Thus, local radio can perform some of the functions of national radio.

Production costs for radio are relatively low and advertising rates can also be relatively low. Most radio advertising relies on frequency of exposure as well as creativity, and some advertising in this medium has been accused of relying too heavily on repeated messages and not enough on creative content. This criticism can be aimed directly at the advertiser as it does not reflect the real creative opportunities which radio can offer. Radio stations have a constant problem of balancing the need to attract and keep advertisers with a natural desire to carry the most creative advertising possible.

Radio advertising has also been criticized for its low impact. The view is that radio is a background medium and that advertising enjoys a low level of attention from listeners. High levels of repetition may either cause this low attention level or may be designed to overcome it. The reality is that radio is an excellent medium when used properly but has suffered in the past from fragmentation and has been seen as a specialist users' medium. This may change as niche stations and improved national availability are established.

Posters

This is another medium which carries nothing but the advertising message. However, it is primarily a broadcast medium. Targeting advertising through posters is possible to some extent. Analyses of those who pass poster sites or who encounter posters on public transport help advertisers to select sites. Sites have also been classed according to their visibility and the quality of their environment, etc. However, these targeting tools tend to be quite limited and require either the advertiser to have very specific needs or to be located in very specific areas for them to be of major significance. (For example, a local store will need to use posters in the store's catchment area and an advertiser who wishes to reach students may find sites located adjacent to colleges and universities very useful.)

Costs include designing and producing the posters, selecting and renting sites and fixing the posters to each site (if the posters include exceptional elements such as large 3-d models, etc., fixing these can be a significant cost).

The medium can be extremely effective and exciting but the message is usually very direct and simple. Image and brand building are common uses for the medium although it is also now common for posters to carry a telephone number or other response element. However, the major response to posters is usually stimulated by the creative appeal of the image and statement presented on the poster.

Cinema

Cinemas carry a small but specific range of advertising. There are usually a number of local advertisements topped and tailed by the agency which has brought together the local advertising. Added to this will be specific advertisements for products on sale within the theatre itself. A small number of national advertisements will also be shown. Some will be television advertisements but a few will be specifically designed for the cinema.

The large screen's visual and sound impact can be impressive and these advertisers all rely on this effect combined with the ambience of the cinema and the occasion to place their products and services in front of the viewers.

Specialist audiences such as the youth market and some young adult and other audiences are reached effectively through this medium. Some films attract specific segments of the population and cinema advertising can be used to reach them quite effectively.

Costs vary from low-cost small local advertising to major production costs for high quality film advertisements. Costs will also vary according to the films you wish your advertisements to be seen with, the range and types of cinemas you use and so on.

Other media

There is a very wide range of other media to choose from. They include the following types:

- Door-to-door leafleting.
- Inserts in publications and
- Inserts in bills/statements.
- Catalogues.
- Telemarketing.
- Brochures.
- Teletext and videotext.
- Sponsorship.
- Stadium advertisements.
- Inflatables, sky writing and airships.
- Trade fairs, exhibitions and conferences.
- Sales promotions.
- Point-of-sale promotions.
- Notice boards.
- Sales presentations.

and many more.

For each medium, you need to consider the key points discussed earlier and make certain that the medium serves you and supports your message, taking it to the audience you are seeking to reach at a price you think is reasonable to pay.

Communication planning

I have dealt with a number of aspects of developing dialogue with your customers. Let us briefly bring these elements together into a planning process which integrates the internal and external markets.

Integrating the internal and external markets

Later in the book I will deal with quality and customer satisfaction. These issues rely on good internal and external communications: any major communications programme aimed at the customer must be supported by the staff of the organization. You will need to ensure two things before carrying out your external communications programme. First, you need to ensure that the relevant staff are properly briefed regarding the products or services being promoted (and any others which are relevant). Secondly, you need to keep the staff informed about the communications programme itself and its expected outcome.

Internal communications audits

The following actions and considerations will be necessary for any internal audit of communications:

- Define issues to be covered in the audit.
- Define the individuals or groups to be audited.
- Define the means of communication to be considered.
- Identify the key messages which should have been communicated.
- Select the methods to be employed in the audit.

Thus, if you are concerned with product knowledge you need to:

- Define what you mean by 'product knowledge'.
- Identify who (in the context of the audit) should have this knowledge.
- Identify the means by which this product knowledge is disseminated to staff.
- Select and use appropriate methods.

Methods will include:

- A review of how product knowledge is disseminated.
- An examination of any literature used for accuracy and effectiveness.
- If the literature is satisfactory, a check that the relevant staff have an appropriate level of knowledge using interviews with all or a sample of the relevant staff depending on their numbers.
- If the literature fails your test or if staff have poor product knowledge, interviews with other staff, in particular the producers of the literature.
- An attempt to ascertain where the communications problems lie.
- If the staff knowledge is disseminated via training sessions, a review.

The result of the audit will be either confirmation of good product knowledge or a set of recommendations designed to bring knowledge up to the required standards.

Audits of this kind can be used to review any communications-based issue within the organization and can be valuable tools for improving performance, quality and customer satisfaction. Changes within an organization can take place gradually and audits are an essential tool to ensure that your communications during these changes have been effective.

Developing your communications brief

While ensuring that your internal communications are working, you will need to develop your programme for external communications. I have covered the details of this earlier (pp. 106–110). However, if you are working with an external agency such as an advertising or PR agency you will need to be clear about:

- Who you wish to communicate with.
- The outcome you desire from the communications.
- The nature of the market and the buyer behaviour of customers.
- The nature and characteristics of your product or service.
- Current and past communications activity of your organization.
- Competitor activity.
- Your budget.
- Timing and other considerations.
- How you (or they) will measure success/failure.

External agencies are suppliers of specialist services and all of the advice regarding managing suppliers applies when dealing with them.

Reviewing progress

Every management activity needs to be regularly reviewed and reassessed. Both internal and external communications need to be subject to regular and careful review. Many managers who scrupulously review external communications fail even to consider internal communications.

Competence self-assessment

1 Who are your most important contacts within your organization? How does dialogue improve your relations with them?

2 You are trying to win commitment and funding for a programme to improve the service within your department. Who should you be communicating with? Who will make the final decision and who will influence the decision?

3 You want to get approval for a training budget so that you can improve your staff skills. What messages could you put across to the chief executive and the personnel director to convince them of your case?

4   You are told to market the services of your department to external customers. How could you use communications to raise awareness of your services in the marketplace and what action would you want your prospects to take?

5   Your department has undergone fundamental changes over the last six months. Outline an internal communications audit to assess the level of awareness of your new services.

6   What are the main press advertising media used by your organization? Who are the advertisements aimed at?

7   Read your organization's current brochures and sales literature. What image do they present? Is this image appropriate?

8   You are recruiting staff for your department. What messages could you include in recruitment advertisements to attract high calibre candidates?

9   One of your organization's most important customers is visiting your site before making a final decision on a major contract. You are asked to put together a presentation on the quality of service your department can offer that customer. Outline the important points of your presentation.

10   What brand image does your organization's product range present? How does it compare with competitors' brand images?

References

1 Colley, R. H. (1961) *Defining Advertising Goals for Measured Advertising Results*, Association of National Advertisers, New York.
2 Reeves, R. (1961) *Reality in Advertising*, AA Knopf Inc, New York.

9 Keeping on track – managing your operations

Why is this chapter important?

This chapter explains how you can manage your operations to ensure that you meet customer needs. It shows you how to assess your own skills and resources and those of your staff to identify areas for improvement. The chapter also provides you with detailed guidelines on managing projects as a method of responding effectively to your customers' needs.

Introduction

At the beginning of the book I explained that what I had to cover would be split into three areas:

1 Understanding your customers and their relationship with you.
2 Understanding what you provide.
3 Managing the processes relating to these two interlinked aspects of your work.

The remaining chapters will deal with the last area. In the first chapter, I discussed generally the role of the manager. At this point I have to explore the manager's role in more detail and look at how you can manage the relationship between yourself and your customers in order to maximize both your effectiveness and your success. I will do this by exploring the way in which you should manage your operations.

Managing your operations – what are they?

One of the most basic aspects of management at all levels is managing the operations carried out within your area of responsibility. These may be very clearly defined or ambiguous depending on:

■ Your management position.
■ The function of your department.
■ The type of organization or sector you work in.

However, regardless of all of these factors, you will have the responsibility of managing the processes under your control to ensure full customer satisfaction and the highest standards of service to your customers. You are also responsible for monitoring the quality and performance of the products delivered to your customers to ensure they continue to meet the customer's requirements as well as keeping your organization's interests in mind. Finally, you are expected to manage your resources effectively to create an environment which enables change to take place quickly with the minimum of problems.

Strategic tasks and responsibilities

These are concerned with long-term objectives and form a basis for corporate decision making. Strategic tasks and responsibilities set the direction for the whole organization, provide it with a clear focus, maintain a consistency across all organizational objectives and ensure that the organization can operate with flexibility.

Your organization may have a mission statement which sets out the corporate direction on strategic issues, and it will be your responsibility to achieve your objectives within that mission statement. As a junior or middle manager, you will generally be responsible for implementing strategic decisions, rather than making them but, by feeding back information, you can help shape and refine those decisions. Some strategic objectives will affect you directly, particularly those related to quality and customer satisfaction, and your role as manager and planner for your department will allow you to play your part in the organization's strategy.

Tactical tasks and responsibilities

Most of your planning will be at the tactical level and will be concerned with short- to medium-term issues and problems. You will also need to manage day-to-day activities in your department in order to maintain quality. Your tactical activities are the link between your day-to-day operations and the long-term concerns and objectives of senior management.

Operational tasks and responsibilities

Your operational tasks and responsibilities are defined by the processes and activities within your department and the staff and resources you control. This day-to-day management needs to be carried out within the framework of those strategic and tactical issues outlined above.

In summary, the effective management of operations meets a number of key business requirements:

- Ensures that you carry out proper planning and manage the operations you have planned to deliver the best quality products and services to your customers to meet their demands and satisfy their needs.
- Enables you to support and satisfy the overall objectives of the organization.
- Ensures that you make the most effective use of corporate resources.

Managing your operations – a closer look

Inputs

The inputs we have already covered include your knowledge and understanding of:

- Your customers.
- Your products or services.
- Pricing and value.
- Supply issues.
- The process of delivery.

Other inputs which have not yet been covered include:

- Staff.
- Resources.
- Location.
- Budget/financial resources.

Staff

A manager's staff are both customers and partners. Discipline, salary, bonuses and economic or market pressures are not the only driving forces which make teams work hard. Commitment and trust, the rewards of team success, personal and group goals all combine to make a team perform beyond normal expectations. Your responsibility is to ensure sound organization and management. You must earn your staff's commitment and trust.

Resources

Your resources – people, machines and business equipment – are an integral element in the processes which transform inputs into outputs. As a manager, you may lose sight of this and act as if the only purpose of your organization is to keep equipment running. Do not fall into this trap. Keep your business perspective clear in your mind and in the minds of your staff. It will help you overcome any barriers to the introduction of change.

Location

Most of us have little control over the environment in which we work. The way in which we adapt to our location can be a significant factor in our own and our team's performance. Organization and management of the environment will also be necessary for productivity, safety and efficiency.

Budget/financial resources

You must ensure that sufficient funds are available to finance the work you have committed your department to complete. The inputs and outputs of any department are seldom defined in purely financial terms, so the resources you manage need to be carefully timed, costed and evaluated.

Your management input

Your own management input is a vital ingredient and there are a number of principles which should guide you:

- **Planning** You must develop and work with clear practical plans which you have written yourself or taken a hand in developing. These plans should have clearly defined and measurable objectives.
- **Control of processes and systems** This is integral to meeting objectives and fulfilling commitments to quality and customers.
- **Adding value** As part of the process of improvement, you should aim to add value to everything you do and encourage your staff to do the same.
- **Ownership** Ownership develops commitment and responsibility and allows progress to be individually monitored and mapped.
- **Investing in people** Your staff are vital assets in which you need to invest. Training and education, development programmes, self-help and awareness programmes can help you get the best from your people. Don't forget that you also need to invest in your own self-development to make the most of your own potential.
- **Team working** Help your staff to work together to make the most of their individual skills.
- **Encouraging creativity** This doesn't just mean 'good new ideas', but ensuring that your team has the support and understanding to take risks.
- **Communication** As a basic management principle, the importance of communication cannot be emphasized enough and you should aim for quality communications at all levels.
- **Make the most of what you learn** All of the tools and techniques you acquire as you develop your management skills should be used

to add value to your department, give your products or services competitive advantage, and improve quality and customer satisfaction standards.

Scheduling and project management

Scheduling and project management can help you manage your processes and systems more effectively, using techniques such as the Critical Path Method (CPM) or PERT (Programme Evaluation and Review Technique).

Scheduling project type work

The method you use to schedule processes or systems will depend on the activities you are trying to manage. There is a distinct difference between new projects or new activities and ongoing activities. New launches have a distinct beginning and an end whereas ongoing activities do not. By treating new systems or processes as if they are projects you can monitor them, evaluate them and redesign activities or tasks within the process or system in order to improve them or deal with problems before the process or system becomes fully operational.

The two best known techniques are CPM and PERT. They help you schedule your project by breaking it down into separate tasks which can be individually managed.

■ Times for the length of each task are assigned and the sequence in which they should be undertaken is shown in a network diagram.
■ In most processes, the time which tasks might take can vary and their relationship to other tasks may not be critical. Thus, in your diagram you may have groups of tasks which may be completed at or around the same time and other groups of tasks which can only be completed after other tasks have been completed.

CPM and PERT are techniques which take account of the variables and identify the critical path through them. An example illustrates the technique.

A company selling a range of marketing and sales promotion products has a field salesforce who regularly make new business presentations. To improve the performance of the salesforce and demonstrate their product range in action, the company decided to improve their own presentations. The sales manager was asked to put together a plan to introduce a new form of presentation. After researching the market, the manager specified a system that would combine colour with flexibility and portability. She also recognized that the chosen system must be easy to use for programme preparation and presentation. By treating the stages from investigation to installation as a 'project', she would be able to get the new system operational in the shortest time possible and have a watertight plan for monitoring, maintenance and training which would help her keep her department working effectively and to the highest standards.

She worked through the stages methodically as follows:

What has to be done?

- List all of the activities.
- Identify all suitable systems.
- Evaluate them against the agreed criteria.
- Decide on the optimum system.

Her decisions were based on the delivery time of systems and training and these were covered in a series of outline notes:

- Delivery of the system takes two weeks from order to delivery and one day to set up.
- Training for input and presentation design takes between two days and one week with at least two weeks and more likely one month before proficiency is satisfactory and reliable (dependent on experience and proficiency of user).
- Training for presentations one to three days with rehearsal/ practice period related to quality and experience of presenter. Initial training takes place outside the company premises. With six sales people, one support/research executive and two support clerks, two secretaries and one typist/clerk there is a need to phase in the systems and training in order to avoid too much disruption of work. However, the system must be in place and operating fully within three months. Hence the need to plan timing and other scheduling details carefully.

First phase would entail
- Order first system.
- Train two sales people plus the support/research executive.
- Take delivery and install system.
- Put together first presentations.
- Test internally and rehearse/practise/improve.
- Test on 'friendly clients'.
- Review.
- Test on real clients.
- Review.
- Order next system and repeat phase one in phase two, using input from experienced users from phase one.

What are the constraints, drawbacks, possible problems?

- Chose the wrong or inappropriate system?
- Staff unable to use it properly, need to recruit specialist to create presentations.
- Staff uncomfortable with it and fail to overcome discomforts.
- Additional workload involved requires additional permanent or temporary staff.
- Costs are prohibitive.
- Clients dislike the system.
- System chosen less flexible than planned.
- A new, easier and cheaper system is launched after commitment to the selected system.
- System detracts or distracts from the company's message.

Notes on the network

Figure 9.1 shows what the initial network looks like. The lines indicate activities. Each activity has a distinct beginning and end and these are indicated by circles. Particular events are expected to occur at these points – for example, a particular achievement or the point at which an order is placed or a delivery is taken. Each circle has been numbered and a list of the events is found below the Figure.

The network was built up by taking the first activity and asking if any other activity needs to be completed before this one can start. You then ask if any other activities can start at the same time as this one and finally ask which activities will follow on directly after this activity.

These three basic questions should be asked as you add each activity to the network. This helps to make sure that you have not missed anything out and that you are clear about the sequencing of the events and the interdependency of activities within the network.

Arrows indicate sequences of events (flow) while broken lines with arrows show dependencies between events.

- If event A is followed by event B and event A has to be completed before event B can be started, that is a clear relationship.
- If two other parallel events have a similar relationship (C to be completed before D), this is also clear.
- However, if B only needs A to be completed while D needs both A and C to be completed before it can start, then a broken line is drawn between the end points of A and C and the arrow points towards D (see Figure 9.2).

The numbers within each circle are not only there for reference. They indicate the sequence of the events to be completed through the network.

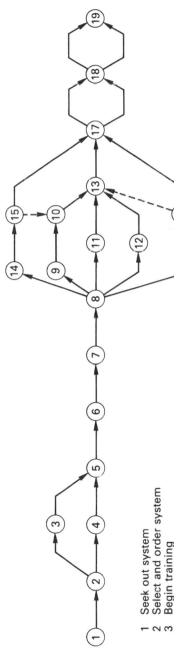

1 Seek out system
2 Select and order system
3 Begin training
4 Delivery of system
5 System installed
6 First presentation created
7 First creation tested in-house
8 Review + decide on go ahead
9 2nd system ordered
10 2nd system delivered
11 1st real presentation
12 Training (2nd phase staff)
13 2nd system installed
14 3rd system ordered
15 3rd system delivered
16 Training (3rd phase staff)
17 3rd System installed/2nd phase first presentation done
18 2nd phase first presentation given/3rd phase first presentation
19 2nd phase first real presentation/3rd phase first presentation given

Figure 9.1 *Initial network*

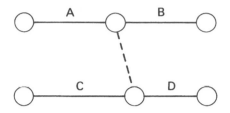

Figure 9.2 *Example priority*

Timings and critical path

Estimating the timings

Make certain that the timings are realistic – not the 'hoped for' times or the 'if all goes well then we should be able to' times. Include the duration of training courses, dummy runs, delivery, familiarization time for individual sales staff, allowance for other duties in a busy department.

Figure 9.3 shows the network with timings added.

Notes on timings

The duration of the activity is indicated by the number on the underside of the arrow (thus, the duration for the activity of is x days). The dual boxes found above each event contain the earliest date of the event in the left-hand box and the right-hand box contains the latest finishing date. The earliest dates for events tell us the earliest expected start date for each activity. The latest finishing date tells us the latest date by which the activity must be completed if the project is to finish by the date of expected completion. The figure in the boxes at the very end of the network indicate the day when the project is expected to be completed. This project is expected to be completed by day 58.

You should use the following simple processes and rules to help you to calculate these timings and keep the whole network logic intact:

■ The earliest date of the event is worked out using the 'Forward Pass' method. You need to remember two basic rules to get this right:
  – Add the duration of the activity leading up to the event whose date you are calculating to the earliest date of the previous event. This will give you the earliest date of the event. Although this appears obvious, confusion between boxes or a failure to be methodical can be disastrous.
  – To calculate the earliest date of an event which follows a number of different activities, calculate dates based on each of the earlier activities and use the highest calculated figure.

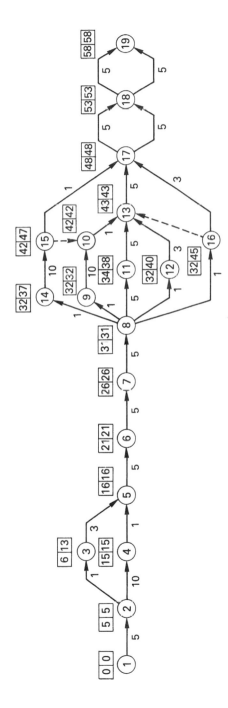

Figure 9.3 *Network with timings*

■ The figures in the right-hand boxes are the latest dates for each event and they are calculated by the 'Backward Pass' method. There are two simple rules which always need to be followed:
  – Reverse the direction of your calculations. Start at the last event and work to the first event calculating each of the latest dates. Take the expected completion date of the project which is also the last 'earliest date of the event' figure and subtract the duration of the activity leading up to it.
  – If you have more than one activity feeding into an event, carry out calculations for each activity and then use the lowest figure as the latest date of event figure.

Calculating the float and the critical path

The Earliest Date of Event can also be called the Earliest Start Date (or ESD) and the latest Date of Event can be called the Latest Finishing Date (or LFD).

The float is the amount of time allocated to an activity over and above the amount of time which that activity requires. It is calculated by working out the total amount of time allocated to an activity and subtracting the actual amount of time required to complete the activity. That is, you subtract the ESD for the activity from the LFD and then subtract the actual duration of the activity from the result.

Table 9.1 Calculating dates, float and critical path

Activity number	Duration	Start dates Earliest	Start dates Latest	Finish dates Earliest	Finish dates Latest	Total float	Critical path
1–2	5	0	0	5	5	0	✓
2–3	1	5	12	6	13	7	
2–4	10	5	5	15	15	0	✓
3–5	3	6	13	9	16	7	
4–5	1	15	15	16	16	0	✓
5–6	5	16	16	21	21	0	✓
6–7	5	21	21	26	26	0	✓
7–8	5	26	26	31	31	0	✓
8–9	1	31	31	32	32	0	✓
8–11	5	31	33	36	38	2	
8–12	1	31	39	32	40	8	
8–16	1	31	44	32	45	13	
9–10	10	32	32	42	42	0	✓
10–13	1	42	42	43	43	0	✓
11–13	5	34	38	39	43	4	
12–13	3	32	40	35	43	8	
13–17	5	43	43	48	48	0	✓
14–15	10	32	37	42	47	5	
15–17	1	42	47	43	48	5	
16–17	3	32	45	35	48	13	
17–18	5	48	48	53	53	0	✓
18–19	5	53	53	58	58	0	✓

To work out the total float for the network you have to write out all of the activities, their duration, the ESD and the LFD and work out the float for each of the activities.

Table 9.1 shows a Latest Start Date (or LSD) for each activity. This is logically the latest date at which the activity can start and still be completed by the LFD. There is also an Earliest Finishing Date (or EFD) for each activity which is the first date after the ESD at which the activity can be completed.

Those activities which have no float (Zero Float) are the critical activities – their Earliest and Latest Start Dates are the same while their Earliest and Latest Finishing Dates are the same. The activity must start and finish on specific dates and any delay will mean a delay in the whole schedule. By connecting up the critical activities, it is possible to define the critical path across the network. This is the backbone of the whole project and if any part of the critical path slips, the whole project will suffer delays.

This critical path identifies where extra efforts must be made and where changes in resources or other efforts will be needed if the project is to be carried out faster or guaranteed to be completed on time.

Putting it into practice

The Critical Path Method (CPM) allows you to produce a number of readily understood and easily used tools which make scheduling more effective.

- Get agreement on the final version and make any changes which become necessary.
- Agree the dates and timings with staff responsible for carrying out the activities. This helps to gain their agreement and commitment to the dates and timings in the network.
- Give a copy of the network to everyone involved in the project.
- From the analysis, produce charts which show the activities, their start and finish dates, duration, floats and their critical level.
- On completion, each activity can be ticked off or crossed out.

In addition to the critical path diagrams, you can also produce a Gantt Chart which is described in more detail in Chapter 12 on Planning. Gantt Charts provide a graphic representation of projects while allowing you to itemize each activity and indicate its completion. (A Gantt Chart is shown on page 169.)

Monitor progress and take action

Managers are often expected to manage more than one project, each with different start and finish dates. They are also expected to continue managing their day-to-day work at the same time. Monitoring progress in such circumstances needs to be well organized but Gantt Charts can help make the task easier.

- Keep asking questions and checking progress, ensuring that the activities on the critical path are meeting their target dates.
- Take account of any changes in circumstances and act on them quickly.
- If activities are completed quicker than expected, incorporate the changes into a new version of the network.
- Check that changes on one project do not have a knock-on effect on other projects or on the day-to-day work of your department.

Assessment

It is tempting to finish one project and move on to another without properly assessing its performance. After every project I ask the following:

Did it . . . ?   *Why . . . ?*

Meet the original objectives?
Complete on time?
Stay within budget?
Have resource problems?
Have people problems?
Have technical problems?
Have other types of problems?
Have specific positive or
   negative points?
Reflect specific individual or
   team performance?
Reflect good or poor judgement?
Identify lessons which could be
   applied to other projects?

After a review like this circulate a report to team members and other interested managers.

PERT

PERT (Programme Evaluation and Review Technique) shares many of the features of the Critical Path Method and can be carried out using a computer program. Its potential complexity and its potential for dealing with complexity can be indicated by its origins: it was developed by the Special Projects Office of the United States Navy to plan and control the development of the Polaris Weapon System about the same time as engineers at Du Pont developed CPM.

The technique is virtually identical to CPM but uses different language and network representation.

- A Gantt Chart is drawn up for the project. On the chart each task is mapped as a set of horizontal bars whose length denotes its expected duration. The bars are located on the chart according to when they are expected to start and finish.

■ Each task in this case may have two or more 'milestones' which are similar to the 'events' in CPM. The relationship between each milestone is marked with arrowed lines, the direction of the arrow indicating the relationship.

■ Timings are added. In PERT you estimate three types of timing for each event or milestone.
  – 'Optimistic time', if everything goes well and the work is completed in the best time you could expect.
  – 'Most likely time', where the person responsible for the task gives a realistic estimate.
  – 'Pessimistic time', where the task could be delayed by a potential problem.

■ The three times are averaged out and the critical path is calculated by comparing the length of time it takes to go along each path of the diagram and by finding the path with the longest time and the least float.

In both PERT and CPM, the number of events and activities can be as small or as large as the project demands. The more complex projects are probably best managed using a computerized version of these tools but whatever approach you use, you need to remember that these are tools and they should be used to help you manage and control and not restrict your team or impose unrealistic or impossible targets. The keys to success for both techniques are as follows:

■ List ALL of the activities.
■ Consult with all relevant staff.
■ Identify problems and constraints and do not ignore them.
■ Discuss the network with your team.
■ Use realistic timings.
■ Calculate and mark up the critical path.
■ Check implications and make any changes and additions.
■ Get the agreement of your team to timings, target dates, resources.
■ Provide full supporting documentation for the network, including Gantt Charts.
■ Monitor work as it progresses.
■ Incorporate changes and recalculate critical paths as quickly as possible.
■ Review the project at completion.
■ Share the review with the team.

Non-project work

Managing continuous processes or systems requires the same commitment to quality and success, and it starts with a question: 'Do you know what is going on in your department?' When you look at something familiar from a new angle you will be surprised at what you see, so ask yourself when was the last time you reviewed the operations within your department? Perhaps you don't do this until you need to.

You have looked at your inputs and outputs, now look at the processes which convert inputs to outputs. Start with the outputs and work back.

- List the department's outputs. Include products, services, information and intangible services such as support.
- For each output trace back the processes which created the output. These will become the processes. Include the staff involved and identify their roles and levels of involvement.
- List the inputs which came from outside the department and which contributed to the processes and output.
- Review the job descriptions for you and your staff and look for gaps in either skills or responsibilities.
- Identify who 'owns' the process or each process leading to the output. Is the owner different from the key worker?
- Add customers to the outputs. Who is receiving your output and how often?
- Identify what your department has done to each input to add value before presenting it as output and identify where the value is added.
- Consider how each output is assessed. What are the performance measures, and how often are they applied?
- What do you need to know to monitor these outputs and the processes which produce them?

You can now begin to see where improvements and actions can be taken.

- Highlight key workers for each output, identify key processes for each and note the links which exist between activities, inputs, outputs and staff.
- List any problems and deficiencies in a process or a department.
- Look at dependencies or duplications.
- Identify areas where there are gaps in information, needs for incentives, inconsistencies or areas where occasional problems occur because of the structure of the processes or their links with other processes.

This will prove a valuable input for the quality management chapter. As a tool for managing operations it will help you to identify the following:

- What are the department's objectives?
- How do each of these outputs fulfil the department's objectives?
- What, if anything, is missing which needs to be added to fulfil the department's objectives properly?
- Where does the department exceed these objectives and to what good or bad effect?

Competence self-assessment

1 What is your organization's mission statement? If there is none, what do you think it should be? How does it affect your work?

2 List the staff, resources, location and budget inputs you manage. Do they enable you to meet your customers' needs? What changes would you like to make to those inputs?

3 'Investing in People' is a popular slogan in companies who recognize the value of training and personal development. How would you invest in your staff and what benefits would you expect?

4 How would you invest in your own personal development and how would this benefit your organization?

5 You need to introduce new working practices or new business systems into your department. Outline the most important activities in this project.

6 How long would each of the activities take and which are the most important? What support would you need to manage the change?

7 Develop a network diagram using PERT or CPM techniques to help you manage the project.

8 List the questions you would ask in assessing the performance of your project.

9 The section entitled 'Non-project work' on page 138 provides a list of questions to answer. Carry out this exercise.

10 Put together an action plan based on that exercise to improve the way you meet customer needs.

10 Quality as the norm

Why this chapter is important

Managing quality is an integral part of the process of meeting your internal and external customers' needs. It works in tandem with the effective management of your operations and your internal marketing and requires a clear understanding of your customers and what you provide. This chapter shows that there are a number of different approaches to quality. However, they all require good people management skills and your task is to transform individual skills into a customer-facing, goal-driven team.

Two views of quality

Quality as a relative measure

Some commentators believe that quality costs money. They believe that the law of diminishing returns can be applied to quality and that, once you reach an optimum level of quality, each percentage point of improvement will incur a disproportionately higher cost. Therefore, they argue, once you reach that 'optimum level' of quality there is no value in improving the quality further. They argue that planning for quality is a relative activity and that what you should be aiming to do is to raise the point where the laws of diminishing returns begin to apply.

Improvements based on this principle contain the underlying premise that it is impossible to reach 100 per cent quality levels without making your product uneconomical to produce. If the expectations of suppliers and customers are based on that belief, you can expect that systems will be put in place to deal with the problems which arise from the imperfections in the system. These systems might include:

- Quality control department to monitor the quality levels of supplies, processes, partly finished and completed products.
- Customer service department to deal with customers who have received imperfect goods.
- Department to handle rejects.

Quality as an absolute measure

Instead of saying that reaching 100 per cent quality is too costly, you begin from the premise that every quality failure costs money and that this cost is too high. You see quality as being an integral part of every task in the organization and believe that quality is everybody's responsibility. You believe that the customer expects zero defects and that your aim should be to make sure that there are no defects in what you produce. This conviction extends throughout the organization as you believe that everyone has the responsibility to get it right first time.

When an organization is committed to these standards it is not only possible to achieve and maintain total quality, the customer begins to expect total quality and is dissatisfied when they find that other organizations (i.e. your competitors) fail to meet the standards. The philosophy of getting it right first time combined with a policy of continuous improvement also helps to keep costs down, and even lower them, while your quality levels continue to increase.

AQL versus TQM

The first approach to quality is called AQL, where you seek to achieve a high Average Quality Level. The second approach is called TQM, where you try to achieve Total Quality Management.

Although there are areas where AQL is appropriate, TQM may be a more relevant and useful approach. Even where AQL applies to a manufacturing process, the organization as a whole can still benefit enormously from the TQM approach. An example illustrates this.

A mechanical engineering company ran its production on the AQL approach. Their products appeared to be relatively simple but they were manufacturing to a very high standard and closely monitored quality of raw materials, standards of safety and manufacturing processes. However, their markets were being eroded by what they believed was unfair competition – third world companies who could pay their workers very low wages, companies who benefited from government subsidies, or companies whose borrowing was cheap and where investment in plant and machinery benefited from tax- and other incentives.

The senior management team operated a continuous improvement programme so that they could continue to compete on quality. However, their sales and marketing teams believed that they also needed to compete on price and were pushing hard to make the production departments reduce costs and sacrifice their 'unreasonably high levels of quality'.

What were the real conflicts? It took some time to convince the sales people that the quality issue could be addressed in a different way. They did not recognize the quality of their own products and they did not realize that, even in a price-sensitive market, it was possible to offer higher quality at a reasonable price. The sales people were focusing on the quality of the product alone, instead of the quality of the whole 'package' they were offering customers.

By demonstrating commitment to TQM throughout the organization, they could offer other customer benefits such as flexibility, speed of delivery and special product adaptation without loss of quality. That gave them a winning combination in key sectors of their market and helped build better long-term relations with customers. They found the idea of managing quality itself in all areas of their business a good bridge between their original AQL approach and the TQM philosophy they were now adopting.

Average Quality Levels

AQL is based on the premise that quality improvements are finite, determined by the limits of the machinery you are using. It is also based on an acceptance by the market that defects are not only inevitable but that they are acceptable within limits. Instead of trying to remove defects altogether, advocates of AQL aim to minimize them by monitoring the processes and output in order to keep the average level of quality to an acceptable commercial level.

The process is treated as a statistical management exercise where quality is monitored and managed at selected stages, starting with the raw materials or basic components, continuing at critical points in the manufacturing process, and finally at the finished product. Statistical sampling techniques together with feedback from complaints are used to identify sources of problems which have caused defects.

The statistical results are converted into charts to illustrate and monitor levels of quality or incidence of defects graphically. A line is marked on these graphs or charts, and variations above the line are scrutinized to identify trends which indicate a rise or fall in quality levels. These trends should be dealt with before they become a serious problem. Sudden drops in quality should be investigated immediately to deal with any new or serious problems.

Customer complaints are handled in a similar way, with levels monitored and problems addressed as and when necessary. Behind this type of control and management is a recognition that a certain level of quality is acceptable and even logical. However, there are two serious problems:

1 The impact of competition.
2 Levels of customer satisfaction.

The impact of competition

Quality may not become an issue until a competitor produces a competitively priced product which exceeds the quality of existing products. Suddenly the issue of quality becomes central and the process of change and improvement in a system geared to an acceptable level of quality can pose serious problems. The manager of an AQL-based system must ask 'Can I achieve a higher average level of quality, so that I do not lose market share to competitors who are competing on quality?'

Levels of customer satisfaction

The second question is 'If I can operate at a higher level of quality, why am I not doing so?' When we begin to look at TQM one of the first things we realize is that quality does not cost, but failure does. If you operate in a market where quality appears to be a minor or non-existent issue, you may feel that it is possible to disregard quality. However, there are two factors you may not have accounted for:

1 You have no way of knowing what dissatisfaction exists within your market. A nominal level of quality is only acceptable where there is no alternative, and marketing on that basis is dangerous.
2 The cost of not getting it right 'every time, first time and on time' is built into almost all AQL-based processes and systems. If quality was 100 per cent guaranteed, would you need complicated and detailed quality control systems and large customer-complaints handling departments? Would you need to spend time on assessing complaints and compensating customers? How much money could be saved?

Towards Total Quality

Total Quality demands a completely different corporate attitude:

■ Everyone must be involved in the quality process.
■ Every detail is important.
■ Once you have begun the process you cannot stop it.
■ Quality must be pursued continuously not simply because you need to maintain standards.

Your definition of quality changes with new demands and with the realization that specific quality achievements reveal other areas where improvements can be made. The whole organization will be inhabited by 'champions' – people who pursue quality, not for its own sake, but because of the benefits quality brings both to you and to your customers. A Total Quality Management programme must cover the following areas:

■ A commitment to quality supported by training and staff development.
■ A clear understanding of the existing quality levels in your department.
■ Ownership of the problems together with a commitment to change and improvement.
■ A sharing of the responsibility and the burdens. Everyone must play their part and systems must be created to allow people to participate.

A ten-point approach to TQM

The ten-point list below can help make Total Quality Management work for you. The first point 'Top down' is always the hardest for a junior or middle manager to deal with because it has to do with the whole organization's policy and commitment. If you adopt a quality programme in your department without the commitment of senior management, you may have little chance of complete success. However, you may be able to demonstrate enough commitment to encourage others to support you. These are the ten points:

1 Top down.
2 Total involvement.
3 Knowing customers and suppliers.
4 Agreeing on customer and supplier requirements; agreeing ownership of inputs, processes and outcomes.
5 Always meeting requirements – 100 per cent level 100 per cent of the time.
6 Agreeing what quality is and how to recognize it.
7 Prevention not cure.
8 Zero complacency.
9 Tell people about quality.
10 Be patient and persistent.

Top down

In an organization committed to TQM, it is not enough for senior managers to set objectives and encourage staff, and make no contribution themselves. Everyone from the managing director to the cleaning staff should be committed and the commitment and enthusiasm for TQM must come from the top. Senior managers must commit resources, they must demonstrate continuous involvement in the programme and they must seek improvements at all levels.

However, if you are the junior manager in the warehousing department of a small manufacturing company which is a minor subsidiary of a multinational, multifaceted conglomerate you may feel it unreasonable to seek commitment from the international board for TQM. It is also unlikely that you have the ear of your company's board or senior management team. So, what can you do about your own department? Can you win the support of your immediate manager for a TQM project in your department?

It may be easier to make small improvements and demonstrate your achievements before you seek support. Instead of aiming for large improvements in quality, simply aim for achievable and sustainable improvements and seek your manager's help and commitment to that Most managers will become advocates of systems from which they benefit. So, benefits may be the way to win commitment from above.

Within your own department, you must demonstrate commitment to quality and act as the catalyst for change. In your own sphere of influence, the philosophy is still 'top down'.

Total involvement

Everyone is involved in TQM organizations. TQM cuts across all departments and all other corporate boundaries. However, if you are the sole driving force for quality in your organization, begin at departmental level and involve all your staff in the improvement programme. You must be prepared to motivate and encourage your staff to make changes.

Ask yourself what motivates each individual. What direction are they taking? What do they do well? Do they need further training or help? Their self-development should be one of the keys to improving quality within the department as a whole.

Knowing customers and suppliers

To achieve Total Quality, you need to keep clear sight of the needs of your customers. Quality improvements mean increasing benefits for your customers and higher levels of customer satisfaction. However, improvements need to be communicated.

A regional automotive components manufacturer won a small contract from a Japanese company based on the quality of their work and had been surprised by the amount of involvement which this new customer wished to have in the process of providing these parts. After some initial reservations, they welcomed the involvement and found that both parties learned a great deal from it. The customer had been involved in the whole process of designing and tooling up for the parts and had offered advice on new practices which helped them produce the parts more flexibly and reliably. Through their involvement, the Japanese company received a better service than their small orders might have merited – with quicker turn around and a greater willingness to make variations or produce batches at short notice. The customer built excellent relations with its supplier and benefited from the partnership. The components manufacturer, for its part, was able to invest in an better quality service to their customers in the confidence that their commercial position was strong.

At a departmental level, you may find that you can improve your performance by working more closely with other departments and imposing quality standards on the supplies or services you buy in, whether it is stationery, software and office equipment, or raw materials and components.

Agreeing on customer and supplier requirements

In reviewing inputs and outputs, we need to seek agreement on these requirements both internally (that the inputs are up to requirements) and externally (that customers are having their requirements satisfactorily met). Both require some research and are likely to require some review of the processes which operate within your department.

The review begins by agreeing ownership of inputs, processes and outcomes:

- Within each input/output process, identify those who own processes and those who implement or operate them.
- Ensure that the ownership of each process is clear. Otherwise, you will have clear directives on the quality standards required but no one with responsibility for achieving them.
- Ensure that process owners recognize their responsibilities and agree to work towards quality improvements in each of their areas of ownership.
- Carry out any necessary reorganization and restructuring, and involve staff in the decisions and planning of these changes.
- Document any changes and review them before implementation.
- Create a diagram showing ownership and indicate any overlaps with other areas of responsibility.

Figure 10.1 shows an example of an ownership diagram. The GSM is the group sales manager who manages the whole team and is therefore the major box or area outlined in the diagram. He has a secretary (S1)

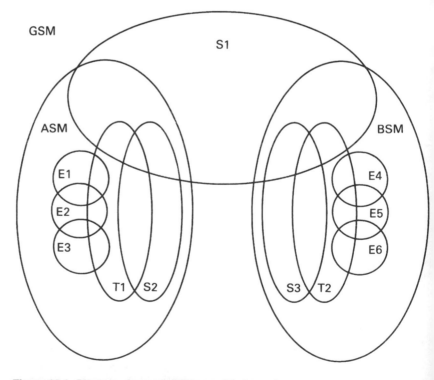

Figure 10.1 *Diagram of responsibilities and their overlaps*

who is responsible for his work and who manages the two secretaries (S2 and S3) and two typists (T1 and T2), and deals with the two product sales managers (ASM and BSM). The two sales managers are directly responsible for the work in their departments and so their boxes encompass their own secretary and typist and the three sales executives. In the case of sales manager A this also encompasses E1, E2 and E3, while sales manager B also has E4, E5 and E6 as well as their respective secretary and typist. Each sales executive handles a specific product but they are also occasionally involved in each other's work.

As you can see from the diagram, the overlaps are quite complex at the individual level, but the diagram can cope with this quite easily. The sales manager then can look at individual responsibilities and map out other diagrams showing the overlap for these too. For each responsibility, he can make the large box the person who owns that particular job or responsibility and then map out the relationships within it.

These diagrams are often called systems diagrams and can be used to help understand quite complex relationships.

Always meeting requirements

Ensure that there are measures or other indicators in place for assessing quality and agree them with your staff. The critical factors are:

- **Quality**   Is the output at the standard agreed?
- **Consistency**   Is it always at least at that standard?
- **Timing**   Is it always on time, at the right time, every time?
- **Satisfaction**   Does it satisfy the customers' requirements every time?

Agreeing what quality is and how to recognize it

Quality is relative but that does not mean that it does not exist. There are three possible yardsticks for quality:

1 Quality driven from within. This is based on the motivation constantly to improve what you do and how you do it.
2 Quality driven by customers.
3 Quality driven by competition or external factors.

The reason why Total Quality is so important and why there is no such thing as a perfect product or service is that the measure of quality changes as situations and markets change. It is not possible to ignore the other quality drivers even if you are the market leader. All three factors must be monitored and reviewed against your own quality standards.

Prevention not cure

One of the factors which drives TQM is the fact that it is cheaper to get something right first time than it is to correct or compensate for defects. A defect may only represent the cost of replacing a product or correcting a faulty service, but it may also cost you a customer.

- Failure has a cost which only exists as a result of that failure.
- Getting it right first time does not incur any such additional cost.

Zero complacency

When your organization or your department is aiming at Total Quality it is impossible to reach a point where you can say that you have achieved it. It seems that you have created a treadmill for yourself and your staff from which it will be impossible to descend. Quality improvement is a continual process and complacency can be a negative and dangerous force. You must take steps to maintain the motivation and commitment to continuous improvement.

- Provide your staff with the highest levels of support. That includes training and motivation, as well as the tools and techniques necessary for quality management.
- Provide an infrastructure for exchanging ideas and information with colleagues. Effective communication enables people to share their plans and aims, discuss how inputs or outputs can be improved, and learn from each other. Communication helps avoid confusion, duplication, unreasonable demands and the constant reinvention of the same ideas or improvements.
- Make use of incentives. These do not need to be financial rewards. Quality awards and recognition by colleagues and senior managers are equally important in motivating staff to achieve the highest levels of quality.

Tell people about quality

One person is unlikely to achieve Total Quality in an organization, so it is important to assign responsibility to different people and prioritize quality actions. As you help your staff maximize the benefits and returns from their individual efforts, you must remember that quality is a continuous process. This means that you need to be constantly reassessing achievements and systems, reappraising processes and redefining your quality objectives. This information needs to be communicated to key groups including:

- All staff in the department.
- Relevant managers.
- Your suppliers.
- Your customers.

By telling the right people about quality improvements, you can demonstrate the benefits of your approach and gain recognition for your efforts.

Be patient and persistent

Total Quality does not occur overnight, and effort and commitment are required to achieve or approach it. The important point of a TQM philosophy is not to attain some mythical level known as Total Quality but rather to keep pushing the quality boundaries higher and further. You do this by constant improvements and growing awareness of what is possible and by achieving what had originally been considered impossible.

You need patience to achieve Total Quality. You need this to help you make effective plans and to implement them properly. You need to nurture and develop your teams and help them achieve their own goals. You need to be constantly aware of your overall objectives.

You also need persistence. Persistence to ensure that set backs or slow progress do not discourage or distract you and your staff from your original objectives. You and your teams need to persist with the goals you have set, recognize successes no matter how small and keep on with your programme. Be confident at the planning stages that you have not set impossible targets and keep monitoring progress during the implementation of the plans. Use each small success and failure to help you plan more effectively and persist with the TQM process.

Quality councils and circles

Quality councils are the key to the 'top down' approach. They have a number of important functions:

- Set the overall agenda for quality management.
- Set the objectives for the organization and its subsidiaries.
- Champion change and improvement.
- Recognize and reward achievements.
- Provide vital support and assistance.

Types of quality council

In large organizations which have already adopted the TQM philosophy you can expect to find a central quality council which is made up of senior managers from the group headquarters, and divisional or regional quality councils made up of senior managers at the local or regional level. At a local level, the quality council is likely to be on a much smaller scale, and may consist of a single local representative.

Responsibilities of quality councils

Whatever the size of the quality council, it has a number of important functions:

- Define the overall aims for the department.
- Gain agreement on policies (and keep reviewing them).
- Advocate and participate in improvement.
- Champion change.
- Coordinate efforts and actions.
- Support teams and individuals.
- Assist with and agree plans.
- Allocate resources.
- Remove or reduce inhibiting factors and barriers.
- Ensure and continually manage communications.
- Manage the education and training of you and your staff.
- Get the measures right.
- Recognize and reward successes, efforts and achievements.
- Support those who fail.
- Ensure that the lessons of failure are understood.

Types of quality circles

Quality circles can take on a number of forms:

- A team of quality specialists who work together to plan quality improvements within limited boundaries or across a number of departments or functions.
- A departmental team led by the owner of the problem or process.
- A team whose leader is not the owner of the process, but who works with the owner to achieve quality improvements.
- A team whose members are not quality specialists, but are chosen to add different experience and skills or to provide a fresh perspective to a problem.

Responsibilities of quality circles

The circle will usually be expected to do the following:

- Review and analyse the process, situation or problem.
- Put together a proposal and present it to the council.
- Develop a detailed plan from the agreed version of the proposal.
- Implement the plan.
- Monitor its progress.
- Report on the plan's results and possibly propose improvements and/or other changes.

Competence self-assessment

1   What system of quality does your organization operate? Does it reflect your customers' expectations?

2   Do your suppliers conform to recognized quality standards? How does their quality affect the ultimate quality of your products?

3   Define your personal quality responsibilities. Can you define the quality responsibilities of a marketing manager, finance manager and a purchasing manager?

4   Do you have a formal system for recording and measuring complaints and defects in the work of your department? How can you use the records as a basis for improvement?

5   Outline the requirements of a training programme to improve quality in your department.

6   What sort of incentive or recognition scheme could you introduce to improve quality in your department?

7   How could you cooperate with your suppliers to improve the quality of their service to you? What benefits would you expect?

8   Carry out the ownership review described on page 146 of this chapter.

9   Who are the quality 'champions' in your organization? How could you use them to improve understanding and awareness of quality in your department?

10   Who would you select in your department to participate in a quality circle?

11   Outline the main tasks and responsibilities for a quality circle in your department.

11 Customer satisfaction

Why this chapter is important

Ensuring customer satisfaction is one of the most important tasks facing businesses today. Unless organizations can retain the loyalty of their customers, they will not be able to retain their business and the long-term future will be uncertain. Customer satisfaction is at the heart of retaining loyalty and it is everyone's responsibility. Achieving the highest levels of customer satisfaction should influence all of your management actions. This chapter shows how customer satisfaction can be measured, managed and driven to achieve ever-increasing standards. It describes the importance of feedback and shows how complaints can be turned into opportunities to improve customer satisfaction.

Types of customer satisfaction

There are three aspects to customer satisfaction which I think need to be considered first:

1 The legal perspective.
2 The customer perspective.
3 The manager's perspective.

The legal perspective

When dealing with customers, we have implicit as well as explicit commitments. It is not enough to attempt to meet customer needs if we ignore our contractual obligations. For example, if a customer orders a specific product from you, what do you do if you are convinced that another product would meet their requirements better? You can discuss the order with them and attempt to convince them that you can provide them with something more appropriate, but you would fail in your contractual obligations to them if you decided to provide your choice regardless of what they actually ordered.

Your obligation may be implicit rather than explicit in this case (where you have no written contract) but it still exists none the less. In addition to the contractual laws which govern how contracts operate between two or more parties, there are laws which cover the sale of goods and services and which deal with what customers can expect and what is expected of customers in return. There are also codes of practice and other, self-regulating, controls which may apply to your business.

The legal perspective of customer satisfaction covers a number of different areas:

- Meeting specifications.
- Contractual laws.
- Sale of goods laws.
- Consumer rights.
- Pricing laws and restrictions.
- Standards relating to your own sector.
- Codes of conduct/practice.
- Guidelines for self-regulating bodies.
- Guidelines for complaints bodies.
- Health and safety regulations, laws and by-laws.
- Advertising laws, regulations and restrictions.
- Tax and other financial requirements.
- Data protection legislation and regulation.
- The Citizens' Charter or similar document.

From the legal perspective, customer satisfaction means meeting specific standards of product or service, price, delivery, safety and quality. Your customers are not misled or left dissatisfied or with inferior or faulty goods or services and you have conformed with the codes of practice and other requirements which apply to your particular activities.

All this however is rather negative, and does not represent a proactive approach to customer satisfaction. A starting point is to turn the negative into the positive by promoting and demonstrating that you exceed the legal requirements. Marks and Spencer, for example, have a refund and general customer satisfaction and service approach which is widely recognized as going well beyond its legal requirements.

The customer perspective

Customers not only have power in terms of where they wish to buy, what they wish to buy and how they wish to buy it, they also enjoy increasing levels of consumer protection which places the burden of responsibility on the retailer or manufacturer. However, much of the legislation deals with what happens when things go wrong and most organizations have strategies for dealing with failures which ensure that the customer does not need to seek legal redress.

The heart of customer satisfaction is meeting or exceeding customers' expectations; at its highest level it is achieving 'customer delight' as BMW put it. Customer satisfaction is a continuous process which does not begin or end with a purchase; it covers the entire 'ownership experience' from selecting a product, to purchase, through aftercare to repeat purchase. There are three clear stages:

1 Pre-sales, when the customer's expectations are developed through advertising, word of mouth or other forms of information.

2 Sales, when the customer experiences how we deal with enquiries and sell products.

3 After-sales, when the customer is using the product.

All three phases will contribute to customer satisfaction. Their expectations during these periods and their experiences will combine to determine the level of satisfaction we have achieved with our customers. These expectations include:

Pre-sales period

Clear, useful information on:

- The product or service.
- Its quality.
- Its benefits.
- Its price.
- Its availability.
- How to obtain it.

Sales period

- Opportunity to inspect the products.
- Attractive sales environment.
- Courteous and attentive service.
- Reasonable and reliable delivery.
- Quality goods or services.
- Prompt redress if dissatisfied at that stage.
- Freedom from sales pressure.

After-sales period

- Support or advice if needed.
- Speedy replacement or refund if required.
- Straightforward complaints procedure.
- Efficient repair and maintenance service.
- Effective customer follow-up procedures.

This book has focused more on the period before and during the sale. You will need to consider all three periods if you wish to improve and develop your customers' level of satisfaction.

The manager's perspective

Your task as a manager is to manage your operations so that you and your staff deliver the highest levels of customer satisfaction. The analysis in the section on customer perspective shows that interaction with your customers is as important as the quality of the core product or service which you provide.

The manager's perspective of customer satisfaction must start from the realization that what you provide extends well beyond the core product or service. Managing customer satisfaction begins with an understanding of the elements which come together to determine satisfaction levels. List the elements in the previous section and identify what you could do to achieve an increase in your customers' satisfaction level.

An important part of your task is follow-up – the period after your customers have bought the products. They do not stop being your customers after delivery or sale and the relationships you build are part of the customers' 'ownership experience'.

Measuring satisfaction

The Post Office, in its drive to achieve high levels of customer satisfaction, has been rigorous in the evaluation of its own service. One of its measures is data on the average delivery times for first and second class post to and from various points in the UK and abroad, information that is used to help them improve and develop services. However, through research and careful review, they discovered that the measure they were using was not relevant or useful to their customers as it measured the time it took a letter to travel from the originating sorting office to the destination office and not from door to door, customer to customer.

They now record the times from postbox to letterbox and have focused their efforts on reducing the time taken for post to travel between these two points. They publish this data to customers with an undertaking to meet and even improve on these times. As a result, the levels of customer satisfaction recorded by the Royal Mail have considerably improved. This focus on the customer, rather than on internal management requirements, has produced results which continue to exceed the results of virtually every other postal system in the world.

The importance of regular research

Regular research is vital to track changing levels of customer satisfaction. Car manufacturers mail a customer satisfaction survey to new car buyers twice – one month after they have bought the car and around eighteen months after purchase. That way they can assess whether satisfaction levels have changed as the customer 'lives with' the product. However, the manufacturers keep dealerships informed on satisfaction levels with fortnightly or monthly reports so that they can respond immediately to any changes in level.

Feedback

An increasing number of companies are encouraging their customers to provide feedback as a means of maintaining regular contact and encouraging dialogue. Feedback helps you find out what your customers really think of your products and services and, more important, allows you to take action and deal with any problems immediately. Rather than avoid comment, many companies are actively encouraging it so that the customers do not 'talk with their feet'.

Feedback can take a number of forms ranging from the basic 'how did we do?' card, which invites a two-line comment on the service provided, to detailed questionnaires.

■ Service organizations leave cards asking customers to comment on the standard of service provided. Questions might include:
  - How quickly did we respond to your request?
  - If we gave you a time, did the engineer arrive on time?
  - How long did the engineer take to complete the job?
  - Did the engineer have the necessary parts?
  - Was the engineer courteous and helpful?
  - Has the job been completed to your satisfaction?
■ Companies who sell their products through retail outlets want to know how well the customer was treated at the point of sale. Questions might include:
  - Where did you buy the product?
  - Did you find the sales staff helpful and courteous?
  - Were the sales staff able to answer all your questions?
  - Did the retail outlet provide adequate product literature?
  - Was the product well displayed?
  - Were you offered a demonstration of the product?
  - Was the product available from stock or did you have to wait for delivery?
  - Were you offered alternative products?
  - Were you given information on guarantees and after-sales service?
■ Companies who want to assess customer satisfaction with their products may ask for feedback immediately after purchase or at set intervals after purchase. Questions might include:
  - Where did you find out about the product?
  - Was the product in perfect condition when you bought it?
  - Were the instructions clear?
  - Did the product meet your expectations?
  - Would you like to see any improvements in product performance?

There is no guarantee that customers will complete questionnaires like this and the level of feedback will be determined by a wide range of factors, including:

- The value of the product and its importance to the customer.
- The quality of the questionnaire (badly designed questionnaires perform badly in terms of response as well as in terms of the quality of the data they produce).
- Any incentive you might offer, for example, entry in a prize draw.

Telephone follow-up

Feedback does not have to be on such a formal level. A quick phone call to the customer can provide the same information and may also give the customer the opportunity to discuss any problems at first hand. There are risks in telephone follow-up because customers, exposed to the tactics of unscrupulous tele-sales operators, may suspect that the call is a thinly disguised sales call.

However, customers may appreciate the chance to comment on the service, particularly if the caller occupies a senior position in the company. Tom Farmer, the Managing Director of Kwik-Fit exhaust centres, puts one evening a week aside to call customers around the country who have bought an exhaust in the previous week. Few customers could fail to be impressed by a call from a managing director.

Customer response mechanisms

You can ask customers to respond in a number of ways:

- Asking customers to indicate a rating for the product or service:
  - How did you rate our service on a scale of one to ten where one is very poor, five is good and ten is excellent?
  - How did you rate our service: poor, good, very good, excellent?
- Asking open ended questions such as 'How do you feel about our service?', 'Are there any improvements you would like to see?', 'Would you like higher performance, greater safety, improved economy or a combination of factors?'
- Asking customers to describe any particular problems in detail. 'If you have a specific concern, please use the space below to tell us about it.'
- Asking customers if they wish the company to take any further action. 'If you would like us to contact you about a specific problem, please leave us a daytime or evening telephone number' or 'please let us know if you would like any further information on . . .'.

Analysing the feedback

Statistical methods can be used to collate customer responses and indicate the general levels of customer satisfaction. The statistics can be analysed to provide information on:

- General levels of customer satisfaction.
- Levels of customer satisfaction with particular aspects of a product or service.
- Variations in regional or branch performance in customer satisfaction.
- Variations in departmental performance in customer satisfaction.
- Changes in customer satisfaction levels over a period of time.
- Changes in customer satisfaction levels as a result of specific improvement programmes.

Responding to feedback

This information is only the starting point. Feedback is wasted if you do not act on it.

- Are your general levels of satisfaction high or low?
- Are any specific areas weak? What action can you take?
- If you are measuring satisfaction with the service provided by a number of different outlets or departments, are there weaknesses in individual outlets which should be improved?
- Are you letting the individual outlets know the results of the customer response?
- If an individual customer has a specific concern, how will you follow it up, and what action will you take?

Recognizing customer satisfaction achievements

Motivation and recognition programmes can play an important role in achieving consistently high levels of customer satisfaction. By analysing the response to customer feedback, you can identify changing levels of performance and reward the individuals, departments or branches who have made the greatest improvements or achieved the highest standards of customer satisfaction. Ford's 'Chairman's Award' programme is a recognition programme designed to reward dealerships throughout Europe who have achieved the highest customer satisfaction ratings. Winning dealers spend a short period in a European city that reflects the high ideals of the 'Chairman's Award' programme and are given their award by the Chairman of Ford of Europe.

The key elements of a programme like this are:

- It should encourage higher standards by introducing an element of competition.
- The award should be given only to the highest achievers, creating an elite group to which other participants will aspire.
- The award should reflect the high standards of the programme.

If your objective is to raise general awareness and commitment to customer satisfaction, a more democratic recognition programme may be more appropriate. The programme might, for example, recognize the people who contribute directly to customer satisfaction – service engineers, sales people, manufacturing staff, quality control inspectors, warehouse staff – rather than members of the management team. This ensures that staff understand their contribution to customer satisfaction and feel that their efforts are being recognized.

Customer focus standards

Feedback can also be used to develop a set of customer focus standards which provide guidelines on the activities that are most important to customer satisfaction. The Post Office, introducing a programme for relocation of a number of main offices, laid down a set of customer focus standards that the new locations had to reach:

- Location in the most important shopping areas.
- Convenient location for parking and access to public transport.
- Longer opening hours.
- Easy access for all customers, including the disabled.
- Space to offer a wider range of products and services.

The same principles can be applied to a professional service business, such as a solicitor:

- Respond to enquiries within a set time.
- Complete specific legal processes and activities within set times.
- Respond to requests for documentation within a set time.
- Publish clear guidelines on professional charges.

These standards are based on feedback from customers which indicated a number of areas of concern. In each case, the organization is showing that it has listened to customer comments and is prepared to respond with positive action.

Handling complaints

A simplistic approach to customer satisfaction is to monitor complaints and report satisfaction as a function of the number of complaints. On this basis, an organization would enjoy a high level of customer satisfaction because it 'only has a number of complaints out of a total sales of x thousand or million items'. It could also report progress if it 'managed to reduce the complaints by x per cent last year'.

However, this is a negative approach and is an approach which is very similar to the AQL approach which aims at an optimum level of quality with only a minimal economic level of failure or rejects. Compare this with the approach of an organization such as Center Parcs.

Center Parcs has a customer feedback questionnaire which asks customers to comment on every aspect of their holiday. The management team who monitor the satisfaction levels regard anything other than 'very good' or 'excellent' as a measure of dissatisfaction and act accordingly to initiate improvements. All staff at Center Parcs are trained to handle complaints in a positive way. They are taught to listen to their customers, to be concerned about the complaint, no matter how trivial or small it might appear, and to let the customer know what will be done about it. The member of staff apologizes to the customer and thanks them for bringing the problem to their notice before dealing with the complaint. Once the complaint has been investigated and the issue dealt with, they then inform the customer about what went wrong, how it happened and what they have done to correct it.

Radio Rentals reply to any customer queries with a letter stating who will be dealing with the query, where the respondent is located and giving a time scale for the response. If the customer does not receive a reply within the time scale, the customer service department follows up on their behalf. This helps to show that the company is taking the query seriously.

These response mechanisms show that it is possible to turn complaints into an opportunity to improve customer satisfaction, but that does not necessarily make complaint management a valid or useful measure of customer satisfaction. You cannot measure success solely through monitoring failure and you certainly cannot develop strategies for improvements with such a method.

Handling techniques

Complaints provide a useful input to the overall process of customer satisfaction and act as a useful early warning system. To benefit from complaints, you should have a mechanism for handling them effectively. The elements of successful complaint handling are:

- Listen.
- Make certain that you understand the complaint fully.
- Thank the customer for pointing out the problem.
- Apologize. Be sincere and clear in your apology but do not make the mistake of overdoing it.
- Let them know what you intend to do about it.
- Let them know how long it will take.
- Give them some idea of what the outcome will be, if you can.
- Do whatever is necessary to deal with the complaint.
- Be as quick as possible but do not compound the error with another error through too much haste.
- Get back to the customer and let them know the outcome or present them with the solution.
- Keep a full record of the complaint, its details, the actions taken and the attitude of the customer after the complaint was dealt with.

Turning complainers into advocates

The pyramid or ladder of loyalty is a convenient method of looking at complaint management and this is illustrated in Figure 11.1. There are a number of layers:

- A large base of potential customers.
- A smaller but still large layer of new or occasional customers.
- A layer of regular customers.
- The smallest layer at the top is for the 'advocate' who buys from you regularly and actively promotes your products or services.

Figure 11.1 *The pyramid of loyalty*

The aim is to move prospects into the pyramid from the base and turn customers into advocates in the top layer. The more advocates you have in your customer base the better for your business.

Another version of the concept is based on a set of scales (see Figure 11.2).

- In the centre of the scales, balanced on top of the fulcrum, is a block representing your potential customers. They do not tip the balance either way.
- Moving left from the potential customers are blocks representing each of the other groups from the loyalty pyramid with advocates as the smallest block on the extreme left of the scales.
- The force you exert downward on the scales increases as you move away from the fulcrum. The manager's objective is to tip the balance on the left side as far down as possible.

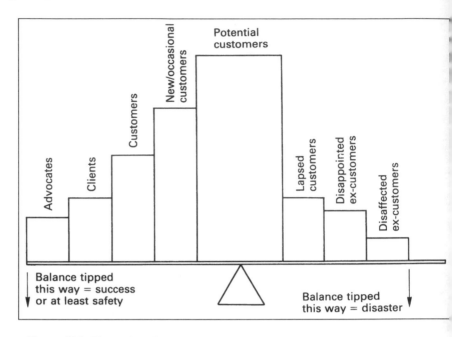

Figure 11.2 *The scales of customer power*

- There are other pressures on the scale pulling it down on the other side.
  - Lapsed customers. Those customers who no longer buy from you. Currently you have no idea why but you do know that they buy from your competitors now.
  - Disappointed ex-customers who do not want to buy from you again.
  - Disaffected ex-customers who are critical of your organization and advise other customers or prospects not to buy from you.

Good marketing, a serious effort to understand and meet your customers' needs, a commitment to quality and good management practices will help to maintain the balance in favour of the left-hand side of the scales and should help to avoid any build up of ex-customers on the right-hand side of the scales. A good complaints handling systems will help you understand and deal with problems on the right-hand side of the scales.

Complaints management

An effective complaints management system should include the following elements:

- A detailed policy for handling complaints.
- Regular training and monitoring.

- Systems in place for dealing with regular or specific problems or complaints.
- A good recording and reporting system.
- Authority for action (as part of the policy and practice).
- Systems for addressing the problems which cause complaints.
- Speedy and courteous response rates – at the complaints, investigation and solution stages.
- Regular reviews of the handling of complaints.
- Accessibility – no one should be passed on from department to department before they can make their complaint.
- Solutions which are designed to satisfy the customer rather than satisfy internal interests (for example, credit notes may be more convenient for the accounts department but are unlikely to merit the same response from customers as a proper cash refund).

You should consider your existing complaints handling system in the context of this list and ask yourself what needs to be done to improve it.

Competence self-assessment

1 What are the main legal constraints on the products or services supplied by your organization?

2 Does your organization have a formal method of measuring customer satisfaction? What is the current performance level?

3 Which of your staff have a direct impact on customer satisfaction? Are they fully aware of their responsibilities?

4 How would you structure a recognition and incentive scheme to improve customer satisfaction levels within your organization?

5 If you have bought a car from a franchised dealer, how has the dealer tried to improve customer satisfaction for you personally?

6 How would you measure customer satisfaction with the work of your own department?

7 What does the term 'complete ownership experience' mean to your organization's products and services. Which are the most crucial areas for satisfaction?

8 How does your organization handle customer complaints? Does it record complaints and act on them? How would you improve the process?

9 Can you recall an incident where you have had cause to complain? How was your complaint handled? How would you have handled it?

10 Draw up a set of customer focus standards for your department. How will this improve customer satisfaction?

11 What training would you introduce to improve your department's level of customer satisfaction?

12 Planning

Why this chapter is important

Planning helps us to focus on the key tasks needed to ensure the highest levels of customer satisfaction. It ensures that we have assessed the risks and calculated the benefits of the actions we are taking. This chapter describes a number of important techniques to improve your planning and takes you through each stage of the planning process.

Planning to do

Planning is an important discipline which forces you to rationalize why you are taking certain actions. A plan is not an end in itself, but a blueprint for action. Some managers avoid planning because they believe they have more important day-to-day tasks to deal with, others strive to produce an attractive document which simply sits on the shelf and is never translated into action. Both approaches are wrong. Without effective planning, your day-to-day tasks will lack direction; they will simply be responses to circumstances. And without action, your plans are wasted.

A well-documented plan provides a guideline for other people. It details their responsibilities and shows what they should achieve and when. Just as important, a good plan summarizes the thinking and the conditions behind the plan. If any of those change, the plan can be revised. Above all, planning should help you to meet customer needs more effectively. It focuses the mind of every member of your team on the key tasks needed to improve customer satisfaction.

Characteristics of a good plan

Good plans share a number of important characteristics:

- They address the relevant issues.
- They are focused on action and include an action plan.
- They are practical and achievable.
- They incorporate clearly defined objectives.
- They include strategies which can be easily implemented.
- They allocate responsibilities and identify expected results.
- They are measurable.
- They are flexible enough to accommodate change, failure and success.

- They are easily updated or revised.
- They include timings and costings.
- They include a summary of the background to the plan.

Structure of a plan

The formal structure of a plan is similar to a management report and includes the following elements:

- Introduction.
- Management overview.
- Background.
- Overview.
- Objectives.
- Strategy.
- Action plan.
- Budget.
- Evaluation procedure.
- Change control procedure.
- Contingency plans.
- Conclusion.
- Appendix and technical data.

Introduction

This should be brief and should state why the plan has been produced.

Management overview

This is a precis of the key points of the plan. It should be presented as a series of bullet points and should be brief.

Background

The background describes the reasons for the plan and provides a context for the plan. The background can include any analyses you have carried out, together with a summary of market and other external factors. A number of techniques for analysing these external factors are discussed later in the chapter.

Overview

Like the management overview, this section outlines the key points and conclusions of your plan. It can be an extended version of the management overview for colleagues who require a more detailed introduction.

Objectives

This section explains what you are trying to achieve with the plan. It relates the specific objectives of the plan to overall corporate objectives and indicates the priorities within your plan.

Strategy

Here, you outline the approach you will take to meet those objectives. Include time scales, costs and resource implications, together with the anticipated benefits in business and financial terms.

Action plan

A detailed plan for each stage of the strategy, allocating responsibilities, targets and time scales for each activity.

Budget

This section should show the total anticipated cost for the project, together with a cash flow forecast for each of the key stages.

Evaluation procedure

Your plan should include key targets and deliverables which must be constantly monitored. This section should describe the review stages and the actions that should be taken if targets are not met.

Change control procedure

This section explains how any changes to the plan should be authorized and incorporated into the plan. It may include formal procedures for notifying other team members of the changes so that there is no possibility of confusion.

Contingency plans

These are plans designed to deal with specific circumstances which have already been identified. One approach is to include a series of 'what if . . . ?' scenarios with an appropriate response.

Conclusion

This is a summary of the main conclusions of your plan, together with an indication of the expected results.

Appendix and technical data

In this section you can include detailed information, analyses o technical data which may only be important to some of your team members. In other words, the information is important but no essential.

The importance of action plans

The action plan is one of the most important elements of your plan. I ensures that you achieve results. The plan should include the following elements:

■ Action to be taken.
■ Start date.
■ Completion date.
■ Staff responsible.
■ Methods.
■ Resources required.
■ Special needs.
■ Impact.

This action plan can be issued as a separate document to the mai plan and circulated to everyone involved in the project. The actio plan helps to build understanding and awareness and ensures tha there is no misunderstanding.

Using project management techniques

Chapter 9 – Keeping on track – outlined a number of techniques fo managing projects which you can use to control your action plan. Th chapter briefly mentioned the Gantt Chart and this is now described i more detail.

■ The vertical column on the left lists the main activities.
■ Beside each activity is a series of horizontal bars against a scale horizontal axis representing time.
■ The beginning of the bar is the start date for each activity and the end of the bar is the finish date.
■ Shaded areas at each end of the bar can be used to indicate earlies possible or latest possible start and finish dates.

The Gantt Chart is one approach to representing and controllin your project visually. You can also use the PERT or Critical Pat Method techniques described in Chapter 9.

Monitoring action plans

Project management techniques allow you to keep close control ove your action plan. As a manager, you are responsible for ensuring tha

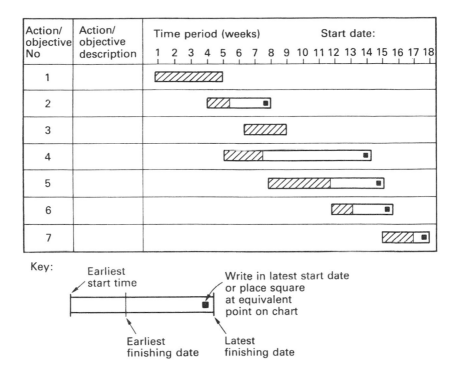

Figure 12.1 *An example of a Gantt Chart*

your staff carry out their responsibilities effectively. Monitoring progress enables you to spot any potential problems and take remedial action before the problem impacts on the success of the whole project.

As well as monitoring progress, you should also review progress with your team:

■ Hold regular review meetings at key stages of the project.
■ Recognize team achievements such as early completion.
■ Provide support if team members encounter difficulties in meeting targets.
■ Discuss actions to overcome problems and involve the team in any fundamental changes to the plan.

Planning is a dynamic process which takes place in a changing environment, and careful monitoring ensures that you can respond effectively to change.

The planning process

The planning document is the outcome of a long process of consideration, analysis and decision making.

Why are you planning?

Planning begins with a purpose which might be expressed in general terms to:

- Overcome problems or barriers to progress.
- Respond to competitive threats.
- Implement important actions to gain competitive advantage.
- Introduce change to improve service to customers.
- Achieve strategic business objectives.

This gives you a broad indication of why you are putting together a plan. The more specific you can be, the more realistic your plan will be. You may be planning to deal with an issue which is specific to your department or which is determined by overall corporate objectives. Your plan may simply be part of an overall corporate plan. However, if your plan deals with a departmental issue, you must ensure that your actions are in line with corporate objectives.

Relating planning to customer satisfaction

As we said at the beginning of this chapter, the whole point of planning is to ensure that you continue to meet your customers' needs and achieve the highest levels of customer satisfaction. The quality/customer satisfaction matrix (QUALSAT) shown in Figure 12.2 is one method of analysing your performance as a basis for planning.

- The vertical axis shows quality levels and the horizontal axis shows customer satisfaction levels.

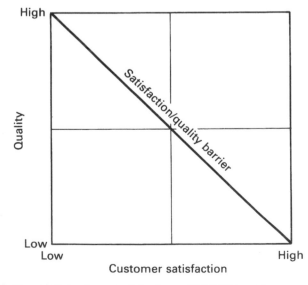

Figure 12.2 *The quality/customer satisfaction or QUALSAT matrix*

- A performance level which sits in the top right-hand corner of the matrix represents good quality and high levels of customer satisfaction.
- The line indicates the customer satisfaction/quality barrier. Organizations whose performance falls below that line need to take serious and urgent action to improve customer satisfaction levels.
- The target is to move as far as possible into the top right-hand corner of the matrix. However, this may raise customer expectations and move the barrier line further up.

The matrix represents a dynamic process and you should constantly monitor the marketplace to ensure that you are performing effectively against your competitors and the expectations of the marketplace. The information in the matrix enables you to check your plan against target customer satisfaction levels and incorporate any changes into the plan.

Background information for planning

Research on your customers, your competitors, the market and the external environment all contribute to the planning process. Planning in isolation, without taking account of these factors, is extremely dangerous. Figure 12.3 shows a simple map of environmental factors.

You should also take account of a number of internal processes which may impact on your plans. The technique for gathering and

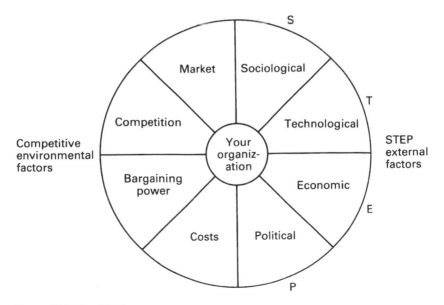

Figure 12.3 *Simplified model of the external environment*

assessing information on internal processes is called auditing and we gave an example of a communications audit in Chapter 8. The audit technique can be applied to many processes and activities, including:

- Marketing.
- Quality.
- Human resources.
- Finance.

The example below is a marketing audit and it shows how an audit can be structured to provide a comprehensive view of a process. Without that comprehensive view, your planning could move in the wrong direction or duplicate something that is already happening within the organization.

Review of the marketing environment

The business and economic environment:
- Social/cultural factors.
- Technological factors.
- Economic factors.
- Political factors.

The market environment:
- Total market.
- Customer trends.
- Product trends.
- Price trends.
- Distribution trends.
- Supply trends.
- Communication trends.

The competitive environment:
- Industry structure.
- Competitive share.

Review of detailed marketing activity

- Sales.
- Market share.
- Profitability.
- Marketing policy.
- Marketing organization.
- Marketing mix.

Review of the marketing system

- Marketing objectives.
- Marketing strategy.
- Marketing information.

- Marketing planning.
- Control.
- Cost effectiveness.

This structure can be applied to any internal process you wish to audit and provides you with a valuable framework for analysis and planning. After you have gathered the information under these headings, you should ask how the information affects your plans and how efficiently the processes are being carried out.

SWOT analysis

SWOT stands for Strengths, Weaknesses, Opportunities and Threats, and SWOT analysis can help you to identify priorities in the planning process.

- Strengths and Weaknesses are internal factors – how well or how badly does your organization perform in certain areas?
- Opportunities and Threats are external factors which influence the actions you are planning.

This is how the SWOT analysis is laid out:

STRENGTHS	WEAKNESSES
OPPORTUNITIES	THREATS

To carry out the analysis:

- List the customer, product, competitor, environmental and audit factors, and place them in the appropriate category on the matrix.
- Even if there are a large number of factors in any sector, they may be unimportant so do not analyse the matrix on numbers alone.
- Prioritize the factors according to their potential impact on your plans.

The SWOT analysis helps you to focus on factors that could affect the success of your plans and enables you to prioritize the activities in your plan.

Defining problems

It is important to define the type of problems you are trying to overcome. Problems might include:

- **Lack of knowledge** You may need to carry out further research before completing the planning process.
- **Environmental constraints** There may be major barriers which you cannot overcome. You may have to modify your plans in the light of these.
- **Organizational constraints** You may need to make internal changes before achieving your external objectives.

- **Customer relationships** These could prove to be a barrier to progress.
- **Staff** Do you have the skills to achieve your objectives? You may need to provide support or training to improve performance.
- **Suppliers** Do they provide you with the quality of service that enables you to meet your quality objectives? You may have to review your supplier programme.
- **Your products or services** Do you have the range to meet your objectives, or are there problems with quality?
- **Competitors** Competitors' actions can have a major impact on your own plans.
- **Current marketing activities** How do your plans relate to current activities? Do they help you or cut across what you are trying to achieve?

To help you assess the impact of these problems and to quantify the benefits from overcoming them, you can use a problem definition sheet shown in Figure 12.4.

	Current situation	Desired situation	Opportunity from difference
Simple definition of the problem and requirements			
Quantification of problem and requirements			Potential gains
Who? When? Where? How long? Details of problem and requirements			Likely time scale
Cost of the problem and requirements			Estimated savings/ benefits

Figure 12.4 *An example of the layout of a problem definition sheet*

- Start with the 'Current situation' column and write down a definition of the problem.
- Try to quantify the problem.
- Write down the effect of the problem.
- Assess the potential cost of the problem in financial terms and in its impact on customer relations.

- Go to the 'Desired situation' column.
- Define the conditions that would occur if the problem was removed.
- Identify who the changes would affect.
- Calculate the cost of achieving the changes.

- Go to the final column.
- Write down the opportunities you will gain by overcoming the problem.
- Estimate the time to overcome the problem.
- Estimate the potential savings from solving the problem.

Force field analysis

Another technique for defining problems is force field analysis; it helps you to identify the forces that will help or hinder you in achieving your objectives and it gives you an indication of how easy or difficult it will be to make changes. There are five stages in the process:

1 Define the problem.
2 Define your objectives.
3 Prepare a force field diagram.
4 Identify the forces.
5 Evaluate the forces.

In force field analysis, there are two types of force:

1 Driving forces which work in your favour.
2 Restraining forces which work against you.

The method of carrying out force field analysis is shown in Figure 12.5.

- List all the driving and restraining factors.
- Assign them to the appropriate side of the diagram.
- Evaluate the individual factors to see how easy it is to make changes.

One way of assessing the possibility of change is to use a simple three-part scale:

1 Change not possible – external factors outside your control weigh against it.
2 Change could be made – additional resources may be required and you must balance cost against benefit.
3 Change would be easy – everything is under your control.

Total	Impact	Ease of change	+ Forces	− Forces	Ease of change	Impact	Total

Figure 12.5 *Force field analysis layout*

You can now give each of the factors a score of one to three. In the next column, you can evaluate the potential impact of the change, again using a scale of one to three:

1 No significant effect.
2 Some effect.
3 Effect of major significance.

Add up the scores in the two columns and complete the totals. The factors with the highest scores on both the positive and negative side of the diagram are the ones you should consider first.

Establishing your priorities

The analytical techniques described above will help you to focus on your major problems so that your plan reflects your real priorities. What you are actually doing is applying value judgements to your tasks and you should use a number of factors to establish your priorities:

- Importance to your customers.
- Cost to implement.
- Technical or organizational complexity.
- Level of resources needed.
- Level of support required.
- Importance to you personally.
- Importance to your organization.

Competence self-assessment

1 Prepare a plan for making a major improvement in the services of your department. Use the structure outlined at the beginning of this chapter.

2 Prepare an action plan for the same project and draw a Gantt Chart for the project.

3 Select a team to implement the project and identify any support or training that will be needed to ensure success.

4 What impact will the project have on the levels of customer satisfaction you achieve?

5 Draw a QUALSAT matrix to show what you believe is your current level of quality and customer satisfaction and indicate your target on the matrix.

6 Prepare an agenda for a review meeting to be held at a critical stage of the project. Assume that problems have arisen and you need to get the project back on target.

7 Prepare an outline for an audit of one of the key processes affecting the success of your plan.

8   Carry out a SWOT analysis of the important factors influencing the success of your plan.

_____

9   Carry out a force field analysis of the important factors.

_____

10   What factors have you used to establish the priorities in your plan?

_____

Conclusions and the way ahead

This book has been intended as a synthesis of marketing with other aspects of management. It is not intended as a view of the whole picture of management but as a view of how the manager can manage and involve himself or herself in the processes of meeting customer needs. It has considered the issues surrounding your relationship with your customers and has shown that the principles behind marketing are at the heart of all that managers do.

There are great changes taking place in management – a greater concern for Total Quality and the contribution of Just-In-Time to improving the relationship between suppliers and manufacturers, with quality and flexibility acting as key inputs into the process.

I have tried to reflect these changes in the context of marketing, quality management, supply management and customer care to show you the relevant skills and explain the philosophy behind them. Organizations which have followed these ideas to their logical conclusion occupy many of the top positions in national and international business, so it is a profitable as well as a satisfying approach.

The competences I outlined at the beginning of the book have been addressed as the key to the whole process of meeting customer needs. Without knowing who they are and without listening to customers, how are you ever going to meet their needs? Furthermore, without addressing the important internal market and recognizing and meeting your internal customers' needs you will not be able to meet and improve your quality standards and the quality of service which you and your organization provide to external customers.

As people are at the heart of this approach I have touched on areas of people management which will obviously be dealt with in more detail in more specialized texts. Here, my purpose has been to emphasize that you are dependent on others to make your job work. The value which you add to your own job will grow with the increase in respect that you show others and with the respect that others show you. Quality without human values is as valueless as marketing without human values. Listening and communication, involving your team as well as your customers, are all part of the same equation.

Planning has been covered in this book as the final stage, but it is only the beginning. I have always been surprised at the number of marketing books that begin with planning and strategy and then go on to look at the elements of marketing (often keeping customers at arm's length too). I did not feel that this was a valid approach here. You need to get to grips with what you do and who your customers are before you begin to plan how to improve your service. You need to be clear on the issues that you face and the sorts of relationships you already have, before you begin to put together your plans. But, once you are on that planning wheel, each aspect of the planning process will begin to merge with the others. Constant improvement requires constant planning.

It does not, however, mean you should lose sight of your overall objectives. Rather, it requires a constant raising of your sights and an acceptance of the fact that management is about managing change which means recognizing and reacting to change, as well as bringing about changes yourself.

In management it is very often the case that your customers will be informing you of changes. If not, the external environment will offer you clues. But first you must learn to listen naively. You must hear what is being said and respond to what you hear. This should help you in your chosen career and add much sought-after value to all that you do.

Index